VOGUE KNITTING

MITTENS&
GLOVES

VOGUE KNITTING

MITTENS&
GLOVES

THE BUTTERICK® PUBLISHING COMPANY
NEW YORK

THE BUTTERICK® PUBLISHING COMPANY
161 Avenue of the Americas
New York, New York 10013

THE BUTTERICK® PUBLISHING COMPANY and colophon
are registered trademarks of Butterick® Company, Inc.

Manufactured in the United States of America

1 3 5 7 9 10 8 6 4 2

Library of Congress Card Catalog Number: 99-32428

ISBN 1-57389-013-8

First Edition

TABLE OF CONTENTS

INTRODUCTION

Does your life sometimes seem like a juggling act? Work, school, and family obligations are pulling you in a hundred different directions, everybody wants something from you and they all want it at the same time. "I only have two hands," you cry, "I can't do everything!" Well, believe it or not, knitting is one of the things you *can* do with those two hands. You just have to be a bit creative about when and where you put them to work.

Mittens and gloves are the perfect portable projects for those with their hands full. They require a minimal investment of time and money, take up little space, and provide the ultimate opportunity to experiment with color, pattern, and technique. Save them for times when your hands literally are free. Cast on before that first cup of coffee, purl a few rows while you catch up on phone calls, stitch away stress on the commute home.

Small-scale projects like these are handy for using up odds and ends or splurging on luxury fibers (most require no more than one or two balls of yarn, so you won't be straining your budget). Use the yarns listed for each project as a suggestion. You can substitute yarn for some the styles on these pages, just be sure to knit a swatch for gauge before you begin.

So what are you waiting for? Get your hands on some yarn and get ready to KNIT ON THE GO!

THE BASICS

Gloves and mittens have been worn throughout the centuries for warmth and protection as well as decoration, and as an expression of decorum and civility. Perhaps more than any other accessory, gloves convey a ladylike quality for women and a mark of well-dressed distinction for men. Many cultures still consider it an insult to offer a handshake with a gloved hand, and of course we all know that old-fashioned cinematic cliché of the slap across the face with a pair of gloves.

Hand-knit mittens have a more playful quality than gloves, and are a perfect first project, as well as a much appreciated gift. Many mittens can be knit quickly and easily on two needles, and since they require such an economical amount of yarn, they are very appealing to knitters.

Gloves lack the knitting popularity of mittens, as many knitters believe them to be tricky or fussy or just too complex. This is not a fair stereotype—gloves are really quite easy to master once you have gotten a few rounds going on double pointed needles. We've made it a priority to present glove instructions in such a way that is completely clear and a pleasure to learn.

There is a fitting Turkish expression said to someone about to begin some handwork, *Kolay Gelsin*, or "strength (or health) to your hands." This is a lovely thought for all of us who have a love and respect for all things done by hand. Handknitting gloves or mittens may just be the ultimate way to honor both your love of the craft and your own treasured tools—your hands.

MITTEN CONSTRUCTION

The mitten designs in this book range from the basic single color with easy stitches, to the more complex with a multitude of colors and stitch patterning. Mittens are designed to have a slightly roomy fit for fingers to "wiggle" around and snug-fitting cuffs to keep out snow and chilly winds.

The simplest of all mitten constructions is the flat-knit mitten worked on two needles with a seam along one edge. The thumb may be worked as a flap at the beginning (or end) of the row with no shaping, or more traditionally, at the middle of the row with increases along the thumb gore. After placing the thumb stitches on a stitch holder, stitches are cast on at the inside edge of the thumb and the remainder of the hand is resumed on all stitches.

The mitten is usually worked straight up to the last 1"-2"/2.5cm-5cm. Decreasing over the last several rows shapes the top of the mitten, and the stitches are closed and secured by pulling the yarn through all the stitches at the end or by weaving the stitches together using the Kitchener stitch.

To make the thumb, after slipping the thumb stitches from the holder to the dpn, stitches are picked up along the cast-on

GAUGE

It is always important to knit a gauge swatch, and even more so with mittens and gloves as they must fit securely. If your gauge is too loose, you could end up with large mittens and gloves, if it's too tight, they become uncomfortable to wear.

When making a pair of mittens or gloves that are knit flat and then seamed, work a gauge swatch 4"/10cm square, and carefully measure the stitches and rows as illustrated.

Making a flat gauge swatch for mittens or gloves knit in the round will allow you to measure gauge over a 4"/10cm span that will lay flat for better reading. However, when a patterns includes a complex stitch pattern knit in rounds, a circularly-knit swatch will test the gauge best and the practice will familiarize you with the pattern—cast on at least as many stitches required. The type of needles used—straight or double pointed, wood or metal—will influence gauge, so knit your swatch with the needles you plan to use for the project. Try different needle sizes until your sample measures the required number of stitches and rows. To get fewer stitches to the inch/cm, use larger needles; to get more stitches to the inch/cm, use smaller needles.

Knitting in the round may tighten the gauge, so if you measured the gauge on a flat swatch, take another gauge reading after you begin. When your knitting measures at least 2"/5cm, lay it flat and measure over the stitches. Keep in mind that if you consciously try to loosen your tension to match the flat knit swatch you can prevent having to go up a needle size.

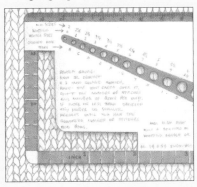

edge and the thumb is knit, either flat or worked in rounds, on double pointed needles. Mittens are often reversible, unless there is a pattern on the back on the hand, in which case the placement of the thumb increases and gore is reversed.

GLOVE CONSTRUCTION

Most of the gloves in this book have been knit in rounds on a set of four or five double pointed needles (dpn). Since gloves should "fit like a glove," they should be knit close to the hand measurement without any ease. Circular knitting gives the fit that is required, and relieves the need for bulky or uncomfortable seams.

CUFFS

Most of the cuffs on the gloves in this book are fairly snug fitting, and usually have the same number of stitches as the hand. Cuffs can also be applied, as are the the the Braided Gloves on page 42 and the Zebra-Print Gloves with a faux-fur cuffs, on page 72.

Gloves may also have longer cuffs that are contoured to fit the arm. The Embroidered Evening Gloves on page 45 are worked with some decreasing, and the Buttoned Rib Gloves on page 51 have diminishing rib shaping. The Peruvian Patterned Gloves on page 60 have flared gauntlets with charted decreases that work into the color pattern.

THUMB GORE

After the cuff is completed, a few rounds are sometimes worked before beginning to increase for the thumb or thumb gore. You can see on your own hand that the thumb juts out from the wrist bone immediately at the wrist. The length of the thumb gore is approximately 2"-2½"/5cm-6.5cm.

The exceptions to a thumb gore are gloves or mittens designed with a thumb opening and the thumb worked as a flap. The Braided Gloves and Gauntlet Mittens on page 54 have this type of construction. The thumb stitches on the Gauntlet Mittens are knit with scrap yarn and then re-knit and joined as before to work the hand in the round. When you are ready to work the thumb, the scrap yarn is carefully removed to reveal the original seven stitches at the bottom, and the six upside down loops at the top. These 13 stitches, along with the stitches picked up at the sides, form the thumb.

HAND

After completion of the thumb gore, the newly increased thumb stitches are slipped to a contrast strand of yarn or small stitch holder. Stitches then are cast on over these stitches to continue knitting the hand. This is worked even from 1¼"-1¾"/3cm-4.5cm

SIZING

Most of the mittens and gloves in this book are sized for women. Those suitable for men and children are indicated in the "Sizes" section of the instructions.

To avoid making a glove that is too tight, measure for hand size before you begin to knit. Sizing is particularly important for structured gloves. To measure, place a tape measure around hand at base of the fingers, just below the knuckles. Keep the tape snug for accurate results.

Hand sizes used in this book		
SIZE	INCHES	CM
X-Small	6½	17
Small	7	18
Medium	7½	19
Large	8	20

THE BASIC MITTEN

These photos show a mitten before seaming. To finish the thumb, thread the yarn through a tapestry needle and pull the needle through the open stitches (photo 1). Pull the yarn tightly to close the top (photo 2). You can finish the top of the mitten the same way or weave the stitches togther using the Kitchener st (page 17). Use invisible seaming (page 16) to sew the thumb and back seams.

or the desired length to the base of the fingers. It is a good idea to try on the gloves at this point to determine the correct fit and make any adjustments.

INDEX FINGER

In most cases, the index finger is the first of the four fingers to be worked, with the stitches for the other fingers slipped to a contrast yarn strand or small holder. The positioning of this finger is carefully spelled out in each set of instructions and follows a logical placement directly in line with the thumb center.

Since the stitches for the hand are divided into back of the hand and palm of the hand,

the number of stitches taken to begin the index finger from each side is usually equal. To close the finger and form a round, stitches are cast on at the inside edge and divided equally on three needles, then worked in rounds. Shorter dpn are very helpful for working a small number of stitches in this somewhat awkward position.

The length of the finger varies with size and style for each individual, and is listed in the instructions for each pair of gloves. Try on the gloves when the finger length is achieved and push slightly at the web of your fingers to get the correct length. You may be tempted to count rounds to match the gauge, but in the case of the finger length, it is much better to try them on and make this adjustment as described above. In most cases, the fingertip shaping takes place over the last ¼"/.5cm of the finger.

MIDDLE FINGER

To work the middle finger, stitches are picked up from the palm of the hand, then along the cast-on edge of the inner index finger, from the back of the hand, and then cast on for the other side of the finger. It is worked as for the index finger, only to a different length. The top shaping is usually the same.

RING FINGER

This finger is worked as for the middle finger, but to a different length.

LITTLE FINGER

The final finger is worked with the remaining stitches on hold, as well as stitches picked up along the base of the ring finger. The length is shorter than the other fingers.

THUMB

The thumb is usually the last step in the glove-making process. The stitches on hold are usually divided onto two needles and stitches are picked up at the base of the thumb with a third needle. These stitches may be redistributed evenly on three needles, but it is not necessary. Sometimes more stitches are picked up to avoid holes, then decreased quickly for a tighter fit. Length and fingertip finishing are as described before.

SIZING

Glove sizing is as individual as shoe sizing. General sizing information is given with each set of instructions. Styles are categorized as woman's, adult's, or child's, and a general length is given.

The best approach to fit is to measure the hand of the wearer. For the width of the hand, measure around the hand at the base of the fingers, just below the knuckles. For the

---

YARN SYMBOLS

① Fine Weight

(29-32 stitches per 4"/10cm)
Includes baby and fingering yarns, and some of the heavier crochet cottons. The range of needle sizes is 0-4 (2-3.5mm).

② Lightweight

(25-28 stitches per 4"/10cm)
Includes sport yarn, sock yarn, UK 4-ply and lightweight DK yarns. The range of needle sizes is 3-6 (3-4mm).

③ Medium Weight

(21-24 stitches per 4"/10cm)
Includes DK and worsted, the most commonly used knitting yarns. The range of needle sizes is 6-9 (4-5.5mm).

④ Medium-heavy Weight

(17-20 stitches per 4"/10cm)
Also called heavy worsted or Aran. The range of needle sizes is 8-10 (5-6mm).

⑤ Bulky Weight

(13-16 stitches per 4"/10cm)
Also called chunky. Includes heavier Icelandic yarns. The range of needle sizes is 10-11 (6-8mm).

⑥ Extra-bulky Weight

(9-12 stitches per 4"/10cm)
The heaviest yarns available. The range of needle sizes is 11 and up (8mm and up).

DOUBLE CAST ON

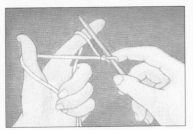

1 Make a slip knot on the right needle, leaving a long tail. Wind the tail end around your left thumb, front to back. Wrap the yarn from the ball over your left index finger and secure the ends in your palm.

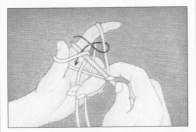

2 Insert the needle upwards in the loop on your thumb. Then with the needle, draw the yarn from the ball through the loop to form a stitch.

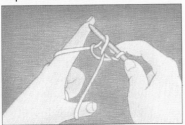

3 Take your thumb out of the loop and tighten the loop on the needle. Continue in this way until all the stitches are cast on.

DOUBLE POINTED NEEDLES

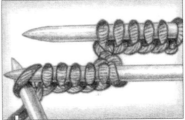

1 Cast on the required number of stitches on the first needle, plus one extra. Slip this extra stitch to the next needle as shown. Continue in this way, casting on the required number of stitches on the last needle.

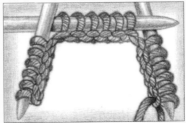

2 Arrange the needles as shown, with the cast-on edge facing the center of the triangle (or square).

3 Place a stitch marker after the last cast-on stitch. With the free needle, knit the first cast-on stitch, pulling the yarn tightly. Continue knitting in rounds, slipping the marker before beginning each round.

length of the hand, measure from the wrist bone to the base of the fingers. As mentioned before, it is best to try the glove on to determine the correct finger lengths. Individual taste and wearing style also determine fit, whether it be a mitten or a glove.

YARN SELECTION

For an exact reproduction of the mittens or gloves photographed, use the yarn listed in the "Materials" section of the pattern. We've chosen yarns that are readily available in the U.S. and Canada at the time of printing. The Resources list on pages 78 and 79 provides addresses of yarn distributors. Contact them for the name of a retailer in your area.

YARN SUBSTITUTION

You may wish to substitute yarns. Perhaps you view small-scale projects as a chance to incorporate leftovers from your yarn stash, or the yarn specified may not be available in your area. You'll need to knit to the given gauge to obtain the knitted measurements with a substitute yarn (see "Gauge" on page 11). Be sure to consider how the fiber content of the substitute yarn will affect the comfort and the ease of care of your mittens or gloves.

To facilitate yarn substitution, *Vogue Knitting* grades yarn by the standard stitch gauge obtained in Stockinette stitch. You'll find a grading number in the "Materials" section of the pattern, immediately following the fiber type of the yarn. Look for a substitute yarn that falls into the same category. The suggested gauge on the ball band should be comparable to that on the Yarn Symbols chart (page 14).

After you've successfully gauge-swatched a substitute yarn, you'll need to figure out how much of the substitute yarn the project requires. First, find the total length of the original yarn in the pattern (multiply number of balls by yards/meters per ball). Divide this figure by the new yards/meters per ball (listed on the ball band). Round up to the next whole number. The answer is the number of balls required.

STRANDING

When working with more than one color on a glove hand, twist yarns together every second stitch. On glove fingers, twist together every stitch to avoid long stranding at the inside.

INVISIBLE SEAMING: STOCKINETTE ST

Insert the needle under the horizontal bar between the first and second stitches. Insert the needle into the corresponding bar on the other piece. Continue alternating from side to side.

THE KITCHENER STITCH

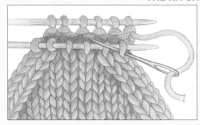

1 Insert tapestry needle purlwise (as shown) through first stitch on front needle. Pull yarn through, leaving that stitch on knitting needle.

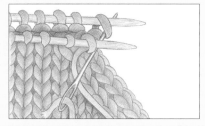

2 Insert tapestry needle knitwise (as shown) through first stitch on back needle. Pull yarn through, leaving stitch on knitting needle.

3 Insert tapestry needle knitwise through first stitch on front needle, slip stitch off needle and insert tapestry needle purlwise (as shown) through next stitch on front needle. Pull yarn through, leaving this stitch on needle.

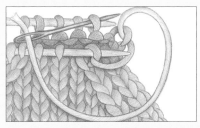

4 Insert tapestry needle purlwise through first stitch on back needle. Slip stitch off needle and insert tapestry needle knitwise (as shown) through next stitch on back needle. Pull yarn through, leaving this stitch on needle. Repeat steps 3 and 4 until all stitches on both front and back needles have been grafted. Fasten off and weave in end.

STEM STITCH

Bring needle up on edge of area to be outlined. Insert it a short distance to the right at an angle and pull it through, emerging at the midpoint of the previous stitch. Work left to right, keeping the thread below the needle.

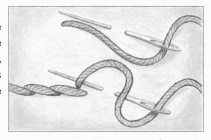

KNITTING TERMS AND ABBREVIATIONS

approx approximately

beg begin(ning)

bind off Used to finish an edge and keep stitches from unraveling. Lift the first stitch over the second, the second over the third, etc. (UK: cast off)

cast on A foundation row of stitches placed on the needle in order to begin knitting.

CC contrast color

ch chain(s)

cm centimeter(s)

cn cable needle

cont continu(e)(ing)

dec decrease(ing)—Reduce the stitches in a row (knit 2 together).

dpn double pointed needle(s)

foll follow(s)(ing)

g gram(s)

garter stitch Knit every row. Circular knitting: knit one round, then purl one round.

inc increase(ing)—Add stitches in a row (knit into the front and back of a stitch).

k knit

k2tog knit 2 stitches together

LH left-hand

lp(s) loops(s)

m meter(s)

M1 make one stitch—With the needle tip, lift the strand between last stitch worked and next stitch on the left-hand needle and knit into the back of it. One stitch has been added.

M1 p-st With the needle tip, lift the strand between last stitch worked and next stitch on the left hand needle and purl it. One purl stitch has been added.

MC main color

mm millimeter(s)

no stitch On some charts, "no stitch" is indicated with shaded spaces where stitches have been decreased or not yet made. In such cases, work the stitches of the chart, skipping over the "no stitch" spaces.

oz ounce(s)

p purl

p2tog purl 2 stitches together

pat(s) pattern

pick up and knit (purl) Knit (or purl) into the loops along an edge.

pm place marker(s)—Place or attach a loop of contrast yarn or purchased stitch marker as indicated.

psso pass slip stitch(es) over

rem remain(s)(ing)

rep repeat

rev St st reverse Stockinette stitch-Purl right-side rows, knit wrong-side rows. Circular knitting: purl all rounds. (UK: reverse stocking stitch)

rnd(s) round(s)

RH right-hand

RS right side(s)

sc single crochet (UK: dc—double crochet)

sk skip

SKP Slip 1, knit 1, pass slip stitch over knit 1. One stitch has been decreased.

SK2P Slip 1, knit 2 together, pass slip stitch over the knit 2 together. Two stitches have been decreased.

sl slip-An unworked stitch made by passing a stitch from the left-hand to the right-hand needle as if to purl.

ssk slip, slip, knit—Slip next 2 stitches knitwise, one at a time, to right-hand needle.

Insert tip of left-hand needle into fronts of these stitches from left to right. Knit them together. One stitch has been decreased.

sssk Slip next 3 sts knitwise, one at a time, to right-hand needle. Insert tip of left-hand needle into fronts of these stitches from left to right. Knit them together. Two stitches have been decreased.

st(s) stitch(es)

St st Stockinette stitch—Knit right-side rows, purl wrong-side rows. Circular knitting: knit all rounds. (UK: stocking stitch)

tbl through back of loop

tog together

WS wrong side(s)

wyib with yarn in back

wyif with yarn in front

work even Continue in pattern without increasing or decreasing. (UK: work straight)

yd yard(s)

yo yarn over-Make a new stitch by wrapping the yarn over the right-hand needle. (UK: yfwd, yon, yrn)

* = repeat directions following * as many times as indicated.

[ ] = Repeat directions inside brackets as many times as indicated.

POM-POMS

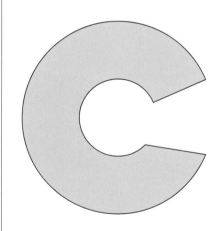

POM-POM TEMPLATE

I Following the template, cut two circular pieces of cardboard.

2 Hold the two circles together and wrap the yarn tightly around the cardboard several times. Secure and carefully cut the yarn.

3 Tie a piece a yarn tightly between the two circles. Remove the cardboard and trim the pom-pom to the desired size.

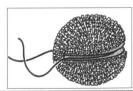

BASIC MITTENS
Chill chasers

A classic study in the art of glove making, these Vintage Vogue gloves in basic Stockinette have ribbed cuffs and an expandable rib thumb gore. Easy pull-through fingertip finishing will take you through this project in no time.

SIZES

Instructions are written for Woman's size Small (6½"/17cm) Changes for Medium (7½"/19cm) and Large (8"/20cm) are in parentheses. Shown in size Small.

MATERIALS

■ 1 1¾oz/50g ball (each approx 203yd/186m) of Patons *Kroy 4-Ply* (wool/nylon②) in #432 pink

■ One set (4) each dpn sizes 1 and 3 (2.25 and 3mm) *or size to obtain gauge*

GAUGE

27 sts and 38 rnds to 4"/10cm over St st using larger needles.
Take time to check gauge.

LEFT GLOVE

With larger dpn, cast on 44 (48, 52) sts. Divide sts onto each of 3 smaller dpn. Join, taking care not to twist sts on needles. Mark end of rnd and sl marker every rnd.
Rnd 1 *K2, p2; rep from * around. Cont in k2, p2 rib for 2¼ (2½, 2¾)"/5.5 (6.5, 7)cm. Change to larger dpn and cont in St st (k every rnd) for 5 (5, 6) rnds.

Thumb gore

Rnd 1 P1 and k1 into first st, k into front and back of next st (thumb gore), k to end.
Rnds 2 and 3 P1, k2, p1, k to end.
Rnd 4 P1 and k1 into first st, k2, k into front and back of next st, k to end.

Rnds 5 and 6 P1, k4, p1, k to end. Cont in this way to inc 2 sts every 3rd rnd until there are 14 (14, 16) sts in thumb gore (beg and end with p1). Work 3 rnds even.
Next rnd Sl 14 (14, 16) sts to contrast yarn strand and cast on 3 sts for inside edge of thumb, k to end of rnd—45 (49, 53) sts. Work even for 1¼ (1½, 1¾)"/3 (4, 4.5)cm or desired length to base of fingers.

Index finger

Next rnd K13 (14, 15) sts, sl rem 32 (35, 38) sts to contrast yarn strand to be worked later, cast on 2 sts for inner edge of finger—15 (16, 17) sts. Work in rnds until finger measures 2¾ (3, 3¼)"/7 (7.5, 8)cm OR ¼"/.5cm less than desired length. (See sizing on page 12 for an accurate fit).
Dec rnd [K1, k2tog] 5 times, k0 (1, 2)—10 (11, 12) sts. K 1 rnd.
Dec rnd [K2tog] 5 (5, 6) times, k0 (1, 0). Cut yarn and draw through rem 5 (6, 7) sts. Fasten off.

Middle finger

From palm of hand, sl 5 (6, 6) sts from yarn to dpn and k these sts, pick up and k 2 sts at base of index finger, k6 (6, 7) sts at back of hand, cast on 2 sts for other side of finger—15 (16, 17) sts. Work in rnds until finger measures 3¼ (3½, 3¾)"/8.5 (9, 9.5)cm. Complete as for index finger.

Ring finger

From palm of hand, sl 5 (5, 6) sts from yarn to dpn, k these sts and pick up and k 2 sts at base of middle finger, k5 (6, 6) sts from back of hand, cast on 2 sts at end— 14 (15, 16) sts. Work in rnds until finger measures 3 (3¼, 3½)"/7.5 (8.5, 9)cm.
Dec rnd [K1, k2tog] 4 (5, 5) times, k2 (0, 1)—10 (10, 11) sts. K 1 rnd.

Dec rnd K0 (0, 1), [k2tog] 5 times. Cut yarn and pull through rem 5 (5, 6) sts. Fasten off.

Little finger

From palm of hand, sl 5 (6, 6) sts to dpn, k these sts then pick up and k 2 sts at base of ring finger, k6 (6, 7) sts from back of hand—13 (14, 15) sts. Work in rnds until finger measures 2¼ (2½, 2¾)"/6 (6.5, 7)cm.

Dec rnd [K1, k2tog] 4 (4, 5) times, k1 (2, 0)—9 (10, 10) sts. K 1 rnd.

Dec rnd [K2tog] 4 (5, 5) times, k1 (0, 0). Cut yarn and pull through rem 5 sts. Fasten off.

Thumb

Place 14 (14, 16) sts of thumb onto 2 needles.

Rnd 1 K14 (14, 16), with 3rd needle, pick up and k 3 sts at base of thumb—17 (17, 19) sts. Work in rnds until thumb measures 2½ (2¾, 2¾)"/6.5 (7, 7)cm.

Dec rnd [K1, k2tog] 5 (5, 6) times, k2 (2, 1)—12 (12, 13) sts. K 1 rnd.

Dec rnd K0 (0, 1), [k2tog] 6 times. Cut yarn and pull through rem 6 (6, 7) sts. Fasten off.

RIGHT GLOVE

Work as for left glove, reversing placement of thumb gore and fingers. (Beg gore at end of rnd instead of beg).

FINISHING

Block pieces lightly.

24

SHORT RIBBED GLOVES

Wrist watch

For Intermediate Knitters

Thick two-by-two ribs give these sporty gloves definition. Easy ribs provide elasticity for a perfect fit in all sizes. Designed by Mari Lynn Patrick.

SIZES

One size fits Woman's sizes Small to Large (7"-8"/18cm-20cm).

MATERIALS

■ 1 3oz/85g ball (each approx 197yd/180m) of Lion Brand *Wool Ease* (acrylic/wool④) in #138 cranberry
■ 1 set (4) each dpn sizes 4 and 5 (3.5 and 3.75mm) or size to obtain gauge
≡ Stitch markers

GAUGE

24 sts and 28 rnds to 4"/10cm over k2, p2 rib using larger needles.
Take time to check gauge.

LEFT GLOVE

With smaller dpn, cast on 40 sts. Divide sts onto 3 needles as foll: 13 sts on *Needle 1*; 13 sts on *Needle 2*; 14 sts on *Needle 3*. Join, taking care not to twist sts on needles. Mark end of rnd and sl marker every rnd. Work in k1, p1 rib for 8 rnds. Change to larger dpn.
Next rnd [K4, inc 1 st in next st] 8 times—48 sts.
Next rnd [K2, p2] 12 times.
Thumb gore
Rnd 1 K2, pm, M1, p2, M1, pm, rib to end. *Work 1 rnd even.
Rnd 3 Work in k2, p2 rib, inc 1 st after first marker and before 2nd marker by M1*. Work 1 rnd even.
Rnd 5 Inc 1 st after first marker and before 2nd marker by M1 p-st. Work 1 rnd even.

Rnd 7 Rep rnd 5. Rep between *'s twice—14 sts between markers for thumb. Work 5 rnds even.
Next rnd K2, sl next 14 thumb sts to contrast yarn strand and cast on 2 sts for inside edge of thumb, work to end of rnd—48 sts. Work even until hand measures 4¼"/11cm above k1, p1 rib edge or desired length to base of fingers.

Index finger

Next rnd K2, p2, k2, sl next 36 sts to contrast yarn strand to be worked later, cast on 4 sts for inner edge of finger, rib last 6 sts—16 sts. Work in rnds of k2, p2 rib for 19 rnds OR until finger measures ¼"/.5cm less than desired length. (See sizing on page 12 for an accurate fit).
Dec rnd [K2, p2tog] 4 times—12 sts. Work 2 rnds even.
Next rnd K2, bind off 4 sts, k next st, bind off 4 sts. Place each set of 2 sts on 2 parallel needles and weave tog (2 x 2) using Kitchener st. Then sew to sides of bound-off sts and fasten off.

Middle finger

From palm of hand, sl 6 sts from yarn to 1 needle, rib these sts, pick up and k 3 sts at base of index finger, rib 6 sts from back of hand, cast on 3 sts for other side of finger—18 sts.
Rnd 1 K2, p2, [k2, p1, k2, p2] twice. Cont in rib as established for 22 rnds OR ¼"/.5cm less than desired length.
Dec rnd [K2, p2tog, k2, p1] twice, k2, p2tog—15 sts. Work 2 rnds even.
Next rnd Bind off 5 sts, work next 2 sts, bind off 4 sts, work rem 2 sts. Weave sts tog (3 x 3) and finish as for index finger.

Ring finger

From palm of hand, sl 6 sts to 1 needle, rib those sts, pick up and k 2 sts at base of middle finger, rib 6 sts from back of hand, cast on 2 sts—16 sts.

Rnd 1 P2, k2, p2, k1, p1, k2, p2, k2, p1, k1. Cont in rib as established for 19 rnds OR ¼"/.5cm less than desired length.

Dec rnd P2tog, k2, p2tog, k1, p1, k2, p2tog, k2, p1, k1—13 sts. Work 2 rnds even.

Next rnd Bind off 4 sts, work next 2 sts, bind off 3 sts, work rem 2 sts. Weave sts tog (3 x 3) and finish as for index finger.

Little finger

From palm of hand, sl 6 sts from yarn to 1 needle, rib these sts, pick up and k 2 sts at base of ring finger, rib 6 sts from back of hand—14 sts.

Rnd 1 K2, p2 k2, p1, k1, p2, k2, p2tog—13 sts. Cont in rib as established for 14 rnds OR ¼"/.5cm less than desired length.

Dec rnd K2, p2tog, k2, p1, k1, p2tog, k2, p1—11 sts. Work 2 rnds even.

Next rnd K1, bind off 3 sts, work next 2 sts, bind off 2 sts, work next st and work first st again. Weave sts tog (3 x 3) and finish as for index finger.

Thumb

Place 14 sts of thumb onto 2 needles.

Rnd 1 Rib 14 sts, with 3rd needle, pick up and k 6 sts at base of thumb—20 sts. Work 2 rnds even.

Dec rnd Rib 15 sts, ssk, k2tog, rib to end. Work 1 rnd even.

Dec rnd Rib 14 sts, [p2tog] twice, rib to end—16 sts. Cont in rib as established for 18 rnds OR ¼"/.5cm less than desired length.

Dec rnd [K2, p2tog] 4 times—12 sts. Work 2 rnds even.

Next rnd K2, bind off 4 sts, k1, bind off 4 sts, pass first st of rnd over last bound-off st. Weave sts tog (2 x 2) and finish as for index finger.

RIGHT GLOVE

Work as for left glove (gloves are reversible).

FINISHING

Block gloves lightly, being sure not to flatten out ribs. Turn rib cuffs in half to WS and sew in place.

CASHMERE CABLED GLOVES

Luxury with a twist

For Intermediate Knitters

Worked in a close-knit gauge on small needles, these Vintage Vogue men's gloves have long two-by-two ribbed cuffs and elastic inset cable panels for comfy winter warmth.

SIZES

One size fits Adult's Medium (8"/20cm)

MATERIALS

■ 2 1¾oz/50g balls (each approx 153yd/140m) of Filatura Di Crosa/Stacy Charles *Cashmere* (cashmere④) in #73 grey

■ 1 set (5) dpn size 2 (2.5mm) *or size to obtain gauge*

■ Cable needle

GAUGE

26 sts and 40 rnds to 4"/10cm over St st using size 2 (2.5mm) needles.
Take time to check gauge.

RIGHT GLOVE

Cast on 48 sts. Divide sts onto 3 needles as foll: 18 sts on *Needle 1*; 14 sts on *Needle 2*; 16 sts on *Needle 3*. Join, taking care not to twist sts on needles. Mark end of rnd and sl marker every rnd.

Rnd 1 *K2, p2; rep from * around. Cont in k2, p2 rib for 3"/7.5cm.

Beg pat and thumb gore

Rnd 1 K4, p1, k3, inc 1 st in next st, k1, p2, k1, inc 1 st in next st, k3, p1 (20 sts on *Needle 1* for back of hand); k6, inc 1 st in each of next 2 sts (for thumb gore), k6 (16 sts on *Needle 2*); k16 sts on *Needle 3*—52 sts.

Rnd 2 K4, p1, k6, p2, k6, p1, k to end of rnd.

Rnd 3 Rep rnd 2.

Rnd 4 K4, p1, k6, p2, k6, p1; *k6, inc 1 st in next st, k to last 7 sts of 2nd needle, inc 1 st

in next st*, k to end of rnd—54 sts. Rep rnd 2 three times.

Rnd 8 K4, p1, sl next 3 sts to cn and hold to *back*, k next 3 sts, k3 from cn (6-st cable), p2, work 6-st cable, p1, rep between *'s of rnd 4 (for thumb gore) k to end—56 sts. Rep between *'s of rnd 4 for thumb gore every 4th rnd 5 times more and work 6-st cables every 8th rnd. There are 30 sts on *Needle 2* and a total of 66 sts after all incs. Work 1 rnd even.

Next rnd Work 27 sts, sl next 17 sts to contrast yarn strand for thumb and cast on 5 sts for inside edge of thumb, k to end—54 sts. Work even until hand measures 5"/12.5cm above ribbing, end with a cable rnd.

Next rnd Work to within 9 sts of end of rnd, sl next 14 sts to contrast yarn strand for little finger, cast on 2 sts over these sts—42 sts (for rem 3 fingers). Cont pat, work 4 rnds on the 42 sts. Discontinue cable pat.

Index finger

Next rnd K14 and sl to contrast yarn strand, k next 14 sts for index finger, sl rem 14 sts to other end of yarn strand and cast on 4 sts at end of finger—18 sts. Divide these sts on 3 needles and work in rnds until finger measures 3"/7.5cm OR ¼"/.5cm less than desired length (see sizing on page 12 for an accurate fit).

Dec rnd [K2tog, k1] 6 times—12 sts. K 1 rnd.
Dec rnd [K2tog] 6 times. Weave sts tog using Kitchener st.

Middle finger

Sl 7 sts of back of hand to dpn, k these sts and pick up and k 4 sts at base of index finger, k6 sts from palm of hand, cast on 3 sts at end—20 sts. Work in rnds until finger measures 3½"/9cm.

Dec rnd K2tog, k8, k2tog, k8—18 sts. K 1 rnd.

Dec rnd [K2tog, k1] 6 times—12 sts. Weave sts tog using Kitchener st.

Ring finger

Sl rem 15 sts onto dpn and divide onto 3 needles, picking up and k 3 sts at base of middle finger—18 sts. Work in rnds until finger measures 3¼"/8.5cm. Complete as for index finger.

Little finger

Sl 14 sts from yarn strand to dpn, picking up and k 2 sts at base of ring finger—16 sts. Work in rnds until finger measures 2½"/6.5cm.

Dec rnd [K2tog, k2] 4 times—12 sts. K 1 rnd.

Dec rnd [K2tog, k1] 4 times—8 sts. Weave sts tog using Kitchener st.

Thumb

Place 17 sts of thumb onto 2 needles.

Rnd 1 K17, pick up and k 5 sts at base of thumb—22 sts. K 2 rnds.

Dec rnd K to last 5 sts, k2tog, k3. K 2 rnds.

Dec rnd K to last 4 sts, k2tog, k2—20 sts. Divide sts onto 3 needles and work in rnds until thumb measures 2¾"/7cm. Complete as for middle finger.

LEFT GLOVE

Cast on 48 sts. Divide 16 sts onto each of 3 needles, pm at beg of rnd and work in rnds of k2, p2 rib for 3"/7.5cm.

Beg pat and thumb gore

Rnd 1 *Needle 1*, K14, sl last 2 sts to 2nd needle; *Needle 2*, K9, inc 1 st in each of next 2 sts, (for thumb gore), k3, sl last 4 sts to 3rd needle; *Needle 3*, K4, p1, k3, inc 1 st in next st, k1, p2, k1, inc 1 st in next st, k3, p1, sl last 2 sts to first needle, pm for new beg of rnd—52 sts. There are 16 sts on each of first 2 needles and 20 sts on 3rd needle for back of hand.

Rnd 2 K36, p1, k6, p2, k6, p1.

Rnd 3 Rep rnd 2.

Rnd 4 K16, k9, inc 1 st in next st, k to last 4 sts of *Needle 2*, inc 1 st in next st, k to end of rnd—54 sts. Work to correspond to right glove until there are a total of 66 sts after all incs. Work 1 rnd even.

Next rnd Work 26 sts, sl next 17 sts to contrast yarn strand for thumb and cast on 5 sts for inside edge thumb, work to end—54 sts. Work even until hand measures 5"/12.5cm above ribbing, end with a cable rnd.

Next rnd Work to within 1 st of end of rnd, sl next 14 sts to contrast yarn strand for little finger, cast on 2 sts over these sts—42 sts (for rem 3 fingers). Cont pat, work 4 rnds on the 42 sts. Then complete as for right glove.

FINISHING

Block pieces lightly, being sure not to flatten out ribs.

THREE-QUARTER LENGTH RIB GLOVES
Stretch it

Impossibly skinny gloves stretch to fit. Change sizes by increasing the yarn weight category and needle size for a Small/Medium, one more to fit a size Medium/Large.

SIZES

Shown in Woman's size X-Small (6½"/ 17cm) using lightweight ② yarn and size 2 (2.5mm) needles. To fit size Small/Medium (7"-7½"/ 18cm-19cm) use medium weight ③ yarn and size 3 (3mm) needles. To fit size Medium/Large (7½"-8"/19cm-20cm) use medium-heavy weight ④ yarn and size 4 (3.5mm) needles.

MATERIALS

■ 2 1¾oz/50g hanks (each approx 176yd/162m) of Koigu Wool Designs *Premium Merino* (wool②) in #2340 avocado
■ 1 set (4) dpn size 2 (2.5mm) *or size to obtain gauge*
■ Stitch markers

GAUGE

32 sts and 44 rnds to 4"/10cm over k2, p2 rib using weight ② yarn and size 2 (2.5mm) needles.
Take time to check gauge.

Note Gloves may be knit in other sizes using yarn and needles as suggested under sizes. Finger lengths can be determined for a custom fit foll sizing information on page 12.

LEFT GLOVE

With size 2 (2.5mm) dpn, cast on 48 sts. Divide 16 sts onto each of 3 needles. Join, taking care not to twist sts on needles. Mark end of rnd and sl marker every rnd.
Rnd 1 *P2, k2; rep from * around. Rep rnd 1 for k2, p2 rib until piece measures 5½"/14cm from beg.

Thumb gore

Next rnd P1, pm, p1, [k2, p2] twice, k1, pm, rib to end.
Inc rnd 1 Inc 1 p-st in first st, sl marker, inc 1 p-st in next st, rib to 1 st before 2nd marker, inc 1 k-st in next st, sl marker, inc 1 k-st in next st, rib to end. Work 1 rnd even.
Inc rnd 2 Rib to 1 st before marker, inc 1 k-st in next st, sl marker, inc 1 k st in next st, rib to 1 st before 2nd marker, inc 1 p-st in next st, sl marker, inc 1 p-st in next st, rib to end. Work 1 rnd even. Rep inc rnd 2.
Next rnd Rib to marker, sl 16 sts between markers to contrast yarn strand and cast on 4 sts for inner edge of thumb, rib to end— 48 sts. Cont in rib for 2½"/6.5cm more or desired length to base of fingers.

Index finger

Next rnd Rib 14 sts, sl rem 34 sts to contrast yarn strand to be worked later, cast on 2 sts for inner edge of finger—16 sts. Work in rnds of k2, p2 rib until finger measures 2¾ (3, 3¼)"/7 (7.5, 8)cm or desired length of finger. (See sizing on page 12 for an accurate fit).
Dec rnd [K2 tog, p2tog] 4 times. Cut yarn and draw through rem 8 sts. Fasten off.

Middle finger

Sl 5 sts from palm of hand to dpn, rib these sts then pick up and k 3 sts at base of index finger, rib 5 sts from back of hand, cast on 3 sts at end—16 sts. Work in rnds of rib until finger measures 3¼ (3½, 3¾)"/8.5 (9, 9.5)cm. Complete as for index finger.

Ring finger

Work as for middle finger for 3 (3¼, 3½)"/7.5 (8.5, 9)cm. Complete as for index finger.

Little finger

Sl 7 sts from palm of hand to dpn, rib these sts then pick up and k 2 sts at base of ring finger, rib 7 sts from back of hand—16 sts. Work in rnds of rib until finger measures 2¼ (2½, 2¾)"/6 (6.5, 7)cm. Complete as for index finger.

Thumb

Place 16 sts of thumb onto 2 needles.

Rnd 1 Rib 16 sts, with 3rd needle, pick up and k 6 sts at base of thumb—22 sts. Work in rnds of rib, dec 1 st at end of every 3rd rnd twice—20 sts. Work even until thumb measures 2½ (2¾, 2¾)"/6.5 (7, 7)cm.

Dec rnd [K2tog, p2tog] 5 times. Cut yarn and draw through rem 10 sts. Fasten off.

RIGHT GLOVE

Work as for left glove (gloves are reversible).

FINISHING

Block gloves lightly, being sure not to flatten out ribs.

FINGERLESS GLOVES

Get a grip!

For Intermediate Knitters

For chilly days when your fingers are in demand, these fingerless gloves, designed by Jenny Bellew, are perfect. They are worked in a simple flat construction knit fabric with reverse purl trim.

SIZES
One size fits Woman's X-Small to Medium (6½"-7½"/17cm-19cm).

MATERIALS
■ 2 1¾oz/50g balls (each approx 110yd/96m) of Cleckheaton *Tapestry 8 Ply* by Plymouth Yarn (wool③) in #11 blue variegated
■ One pair each sizes 4 and 6 (3.5 and 4mm) needles *or size to obtain gauge*
■ Stitch markers

GAUGE
22 sts and 30 rows to 4"/10cm over St st using larger needles.
Take time to check gauge.

RIGHT GLOVE
With smaller needles, cast on 40 sts. Beg on WS, k 1 row, p 1 row, k 1 row. Change to larger needles. [K 1 row, p 1 row] 5 times.

Thumb gore
Next row K20, pm, inc 1 st in next st, k2, inc 1 st in next st, pm, k16—42 sts. Work 3 rows even.
Inc row K20, sl marker, inc 1 st in next st, k to 1 st before 2nd marker, inc 1 st in next st, sl marker, k to end—44 sts. Work 3 rows even. Rep between *'s 3 times more. Rep inc row—52 sts. P 1 row.

Thumb
Next row K34, turn.
Next row P12, turn.
Next row (RS) Cast on 3 sts, for inside edge

of thumb, k next 12 sts—15 sts. Work 3 more rows on these 15 sts. P 1 row, k 1 row, p 1 row. Bind off loosely knitwise.

Hand
Rejoin yarn at base of 3 cast-on sts of thumb and pick up and k 3 sts in these sts, k to end. Cont in St st on these 43 sts for 1½"/4cm more, dec 1 st at center of last row—42 sts.

Index finger
Next row K27, turn.
Next row P12, turn.
Next row Cast on 2 sts for inside edge of finger, k next 12 sts—14 sts. Complete as for thumb.

Middle finger
Join yarn at base of cast-on sts and pick up and k 2 sts in these sts at base of index finger, k5, turn.
Next row P12, turn.
Next row Cast on 2 sts, then cont on 14 sts and complete as for index finger.

Ring finger
Work as for middle finger.

Little finger
Join yarn at base of cast-on sts and pick up and k 2 sts in these sts at base of ring finger, k5, turn.
Next row P12. Cont on 12 sts and complete as for other fingers.

LEFT GLOVE
Work as for right glove to thumb gore.

Thumb gore
Next row K16, pm, inc 1 st in next st, k2, inc 1 st in next st, pm, k20—42 sts. Cont as for right glove to thumb.

Thumb
Next row K31, turn. Then cont as for right glove.

FINISHING
Block pieces lightly. Sew side seam, thumb and finger seams.

For the great outdoors. Bulky-knit mittens have an expandable ribbed thumb gore and separate index finger for extra dexterity. Designed by Diane Zangl.

SIZES

Instructions are written for Adult's size Medium (7½"/19cm). Changes for sizes Large (8"/20cm) and X-Large (9"/23cm) are in parentheses. Shown in size Medium.

MATERIALS

■ 1 8oz/250g hank (approx 310yd/286m) of Wool Pak Yarns NZ/Baabajoes Wool Co. *14 Ply* (wool⑤) in nutmeg
■ 1 set (4) dpn size 6 (4mm) *or size to obtain gauge*
■ Stitch markers

GAUGE

18 sts and 24 rnds to 4"/10cm over St st using size 6 (4mm) needles.
Take time to check gauge.

TWISTED RIB PATTERN

(even number of sts)
Rnd 1 *K1 tbl, p1; rep from * around.
Rep rnd 1 for twisted rib pat.

LEFT MITTEN

With size 6 (4mm) needles, cast on 30 (32, 36) sts. Divide sts onto 3 needles as foll: 10 (10, 12) sts on *Needle 1*; 10 (12, 12) sts on *Needle 2*; 10 (10, 12) sts on *Needle 3*. Join, taking care not to twist sts on needles. Mark end of rnd and sl marker every rnd. Work in rnds of twisted rib pat for 3"/7.5cm, inc 4 sts evenly on last rnd—34 (36, 40) sts.

Thumb gore

Next rnd K3, p1, pm, k3, pm, p1, k to end.
Inc rnd K3, p1, sl marker, insert RH needle into st one row below next st on needle and k this st (inc), k to 1 st before 2nd marker, work

inc, sl marker, p1, k to end. Work 2 rnds even. Rep these 3 rnds 3 (3, 4) times more. Rep inc rnd—13 (13, 15) sts between markers for thumb.
Next rnd K4, sl next 13 (13, 15) sts to contrast yarn strand and cast on 3 sts for inside edge of thumb, k to end of rnd—34 (36, 40) sts. Work even for 1½ (1¾, 2)"/4 (4.5, 5)cm or until desired length to base of fingers.

Index finger

Next rnd K10 (10, 12), sl rem sts to contrast yarn strand to be worked later, cast on 3 sts for inner edge of finger—13 (13, 15) sts. Redistribute sts evenly on 3 needles. Join and work in rnds until finger measures 2½ (2¾, 3)"/6.5 (7, 7.5)cm.
Dec rnd K1, [k2tog] 6 (6, 7) times. Cut yarn and draw through rem 7 (7, 8) sts. Fasten off.

Hand

Sl 12 (13, 14) sts onto *Needle 1* and k these sts, with *Needle 2*, pick up and k 4 sts at base of index finger, with *Needle 3*, k rem 12 (13, 14) sts—28 (30, 32) sts. Join and work in rnds for 3 (3, 3½)"/7.5 (7.5, 9)cm more.
Dec rnd [K2tog] 14 (15, 16) times. K 1 rnd.
Dec rnd K0 (1, 0), k2tog 7 (7, 8) times. Cut yarn and draw through rem 7 (8, 8) sts. Fasten off.

Thumb

Place 13 (13, 15) sts of thumb onto 2 needles.
Rnd 1 K13 (13, 15), with 3rd needle, pick up and k 2 sts at base of thumb—15 (15, 17) sts. Join and work in rnds for 2 (2, 2½)"/5 (5, 6.5)cm.
Next rnd K1, [k2tog] 7 (7, 8) times. Cut yarn and draw through rem 8 (8, 9) sts. Fasten off.

RIGHT MITTEN

Work as for left mitten (reversible).

FINISHING

Block mittens lightly.

TURKISH PATTERN MITTENS

Anatolian handcraft

For Experienced Knitters

Turkish sock patterns inspired these colorful mittens, knit from cuff to pointed top. The pattern in the cuff shows the hook (Çengel) symbol, sometimes interpreted as a hook to hold the heart; the hand pattern comes from a design based on an earring (Küpeli). Designed by E.J. Slayton.

SIZES
Instructions are written for Woman's size Small/Medium—S/M (7"-7½"/18cm-19cm). Changes for Large—L (8"/20cm) are in parentheses. Shown in size Large.

MATERIALS
■ 1 3½oz/100g ball (each approx 218yd/ 200m) of K1C2 *Parfait Solids* (wool③) in #1730 plum (A)
■ 2 1¾oz/50g ball (each approx 109yd/ 100m) of *Parfait Swirls* (wool③) in #4111 beige heather (B)
■ One set (4) each dpn sizes 5 and 6 (3.75 and 4mm) *or size to obtain gauge*
■ Stitch holders and markers

GAUGE
24 sts and 24 rnds to 4"/10cm over St st and chart pats using larger needles.
Take time to check gauge.

Notes 1) To inc foll chart, insert RH needle into st one row below next st on needle and k this st (inc). **2)** If making smaller size, omit sts indicated with an arrow at lower edge of hand chart.

RIGHT MITTEN
With smaller needles and B, cast on 56 sts. Divide sts onto 3 needles. Join, taking care not to twist sts on needles. Mark end of rnd and sl marker every rnd. K 3 rnds.

Next rnd Bring yarn to front, sl first st of next rnd, take yarn to back, place slipped st back to LH needle (wrap made). Turn work around so that purl side is facing and to work in opposite direction. K 1 rnd, working last st and wrap tog. Divide sts onto 3 needles as foll: 28 sts on *Needle 1* and 14 sts on each of *Needles 2 and 3*. Change to larger dpn and k 2 rnds with A.

Beg cuff chart
Foll chart from right to left, work rnds 1-20 foll chart. Change to smaller dpn.
Rnd 21 With B, k as foll: *Needle 1*, Dec 6 (4) sts evenly spaced; *Needle 2,* Dec 3 (2) sts evenly spaced; *Needle 3,* Dec 3 (2) sts evenly spaced. There are 22 (24) sts on *Needle 1* and 11 (12) sts on each of *Needles 2 and 3*. With B, purl 44 (48) sts.

Beg hand chart
Beg with rnd 7 (1), omitting sts on chart as indicated for size S/M and working all 48 sts for size L, work sts 1-24 for back of hand (*Needle 1*) and sts 25-48 for palm of hand (*Needles 2 and 3*). Cont to foll chart in this way through rnd 10 (4).
Rnd 11 (5) Work sts of *Needle 1*; work to thumb placement (first x on chart), pm, inc 1 A st, k1 B, inc 1 A st, pm, work to end. Work 1 rnd even. Cont in pat foll chart (and working inc sts into pat foll thumb chart), inc 1 st every other rnd after first marker and before 2nd marker until there are 15 sts between markers. Inc 1 st in pat on next rnd for complete pat rep (see thumb chart)—16 sts.

Hand
Next rnd Work to marker, sl 16 sts for thumb to holder and cast on 1 st for inside of thumb, work to end—44 (48) sts. Cont in pat foll hand chart through rnd 55.

Top shaping

Rnd 56 On *Needle 1*, K1 A, with B, ssk, work to last 2 sts of *Needle 1*, with B, k2tog; on *Needle 2*, K1 A, with B, ssk, work to end of *Needle 2*; on *Needle 3*, Work to last 2 sts of *Needle 3*, with B, k2tog. Cont to dec 4 sts in this way (see chart) every rnd until 8 sts rem. Cut yarn and draw through rem 8 sts. Fasten off.

Thumb

Place 16 sts of thumb onto 2 needles.

Rnd 1 K16, with 3rd needle, pick up and k 2 sts at base of thumb.

Next rnd Work in pat, dec 2 sts so that 16 sts rem for thumb pat. Cont foll thumb chart until thumb measures 2¾"/7cm.

Next rnd With A, [k2tog] 8 times. Finish as for top of mitten.

LEFT MITTEN

Work as for right mitten, reversing thumb placement as foll: work to 2nd x on chart on rnd 11 (5), or the 3rd (4th) st from end of palm.

FINISHING

Block pieces lightly.

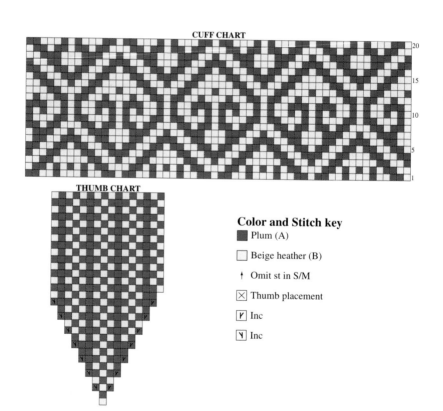

CUFF CHART

THUMB CHART

Color and Stitch key

■ Plum (A)

☐ Beige heather (B)

† Omit st in S/M

☒ Thumb placement

Ⴑ Inc

Ⴑ Inc

HAND CHART

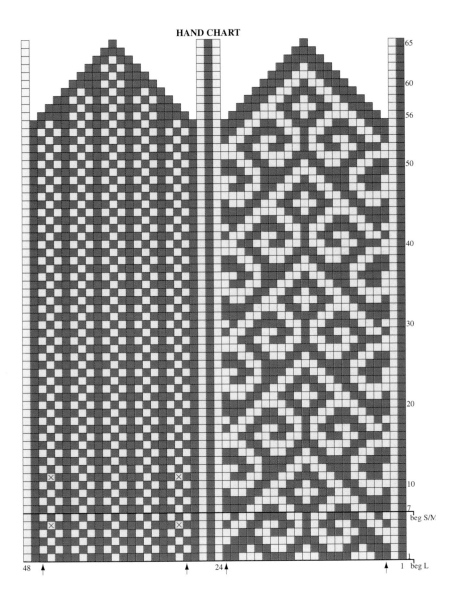

BRAIDED GLOVES

Off the cuff

As heavenly to knit as they are to wear, these angora-blend gloves are finished with braided knit cuffs. The thumb is knit as a flap instead of the traditional thumb gore. Designed by Vickie F.C.

SIZES
One size fits Woman's size Small-Medium (7"-7½"/18cm-19cm).

MATERIALS
■ 2 .87oz/25g balls (each approx 108yd/100m) of Tahki *Jolie* (angora/wool④) in #5005 lt blue (MC)
■ 1 1¾oz/50g ball (each approx 140yd/135m) of Tahki *Sable* (wool/angora④) in #1643 blue (CC)
■ 1 set (4) each dpn sizes 4 and 6 (3.5 and 4mm) *or size to obtain gauge*

GAUGE
27 sts and 36 rnds to 4"/10cm over St st using larger needles and MC.
Take time to check gauge.

LEFT GLOVE
With smaller dpn and MC, cast on 48 sts. Divide 16 sts onto each of 3 needles. Join, taking care not to twist sts on needles. Mark end of rnd and sl marker every rnd.
Rnd 1 *K1, p1; rep from * around. Cont in k1, p1 rib for 1¼"/3cm. Change to larger dpn and k next rnd, inc 2 sts evenly spaced—50 sts. Work even for 2"/5cm above ribbing.

Thumb opening
Next rnd K to last 10 sts of rnd, k8 and sl these sts to a contrast yarn strand for thumb, cast on 8 sts over these sts for other side of thumb, k to end of rnd. Cont in St st

on all 50 sts for 2½"/6.5cm more or until desired length to base of fingers.

Index finger
Next rnd K6, sl next 38 sts to contrast yarn strand to be worked later, cast on 2 sts for inner edge of finger, k rem 6 sts—14 sts. Work in rnds until finger measures 3"/7.5cm OR ¼"/.5cm less than desired length. (See sizing on page 12 for an accurate fit).
Dec rnd [K2tog, k1] 4 times, k2tog—9 sts. K 1 rnd.
Dec rnd [K1, k2tog] 3 times—6 sts. Weave sts tog using Kitchener st.

Middle finger
Sl 7 sts from palm of hand to dpn, k these sts, then pick up and k 1 st at base of index finger, k7 sts from back of hand, cast on 1 st at end—16 sts. Work in rnds until finger measures 3½"/9cm.
Dec rnd K1, [k2tog, k1] 5 times—11 sts. K 1 rnd.
Dec rnd [K1, k2tog] 3 times, k2—8 sts. Weave sts tog using Kitchener st.

Ring finger
Work as for middle finger for 3¼"/8.5cm. Complete as for middle finger.

Little finger
Sl 5 sts from palm of hand to dpn, k these sts then pick up and k 2 sts at base of ring finger, k5 from back of hand—12 sts. Work in rnds until finger measures 2½"/6.5cm.
Dec rnd [K1, k2tog] 4 times—8 sts. K 1 rnd.
Dec rnd [K2tog] 4 times. Weave sts tog using Kitchener st.

Thumb
K the 8 sts from holder for thumb, pick up and k 8 sts in cast-on sts at base of thumb—

16 sts. Work in rnds until thumb measures 2¾"/7cm. Complete as for middle finger.

Braided cuff

With larger needles and MC, cast on 10 sts. Work in St st for 12"/30.5cm. Bind off. Work 2 more bands in same way with CC. Braid three bands tog and sew around rib cuff, sewing seam at center of palm.

RIGHT GLOVE

Work as for left glove to thumb opening.
Next rnd K2, k8 and sl these sts to contrast yarn strand for thumb, cast on 8 sts over these sts and k to end. Cont as for left glove, reversing finger placement.

FINISHING

Block gloves lightly.

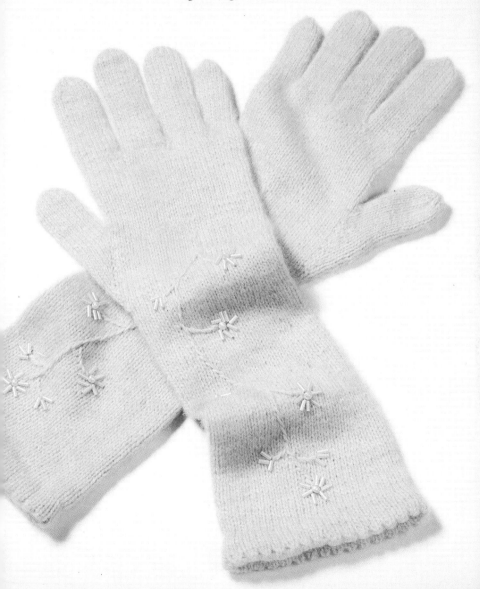

Opera-length cashmere gloves with picot-turned cuffs are embroidered with stem stitch, bugle beads, and seed pearls. Designed by Nicky Epstein.

SIZES

One size fits Woman's size Medium-Large (7½"-8"/19cm-20cm).

MATERIALS

▪ 3 .88oz/25g balls (each approx 124yd/115m) of Lang/Berroco *Cashmere Premium* (cashmere③) in #7894 cream
▪ One set (4) dpn size 2 (2.5mm) *or size to obtain gauge*
▪ 9 dozen 6mm pearl bugle beads
▪ 1 dozen size 4.5mm seed pearls
▪ Matching thread
▪ Disappearing maker

GAUGE

28 sts and 40 rnds to 4"/10cm over St st using size 2 (2.5mm) needles.
Take time to check gauge.

RIGHT GLOVE

Cast on 61 sts. Divide sts evenly onto 3 needles. Join, taking care not to twist sts on needles. Mark end of rnd and sl marker every rnd. K 5 rnds.

Picot rnd K1, *yo, k2tog; rep from * around. Cont in St st, dec 1 st at end of every 10th rnd (2 sts before marker) 7 times—54 sts. Work even until piece measures 8½"/21.5cm from picot rnd.

Thumb gore

Rnd 1 K29, p1, M1, k1, M1, p1, k to end. K 2 rnds.
Rnd 4 K29, p1, M1, k3, M1, p1, k to end. Cont in this way to inc 2 sts every 3rd rnd by M1 st after first p1 and before 2nd p1 until there are a total of 68 sts. K 3 rnds.
Next rnd K30, sl next 15 sts to contrast yarn strand and cast on 3 sts for inside edge of thumb, k to end—56 sts. Work even for 2"/5cm more or desired length to base of fingers.

Index finger

K23 sts and sl to contrast yarn strand, k16, cast on 2 sts for inner edge of finger and sl rem 17 sts to other end of yarn strand. Join and work in rnds on 18 sts until finger measures 3"/7.5cm OR ¼"/.5cm less than desired length. (See sizing on page 12 for an accurate fit).
Dec rnd [K2tog] 9 times. K 1 rnd.

Dec rnd [K1, k2tog] 3 times—6 sts. Weave sts tog using Kitchener st.

Middle finger
Sl 6 sts from back of hand to dpn, k these sts then pick up and k 2 sts at base of index finger, k8 sts from palm of hand, cast on 2 sts at end—18 sts. Complete as for index finger, working until finger measures 3½"/9cm.

Ring finger
Work as for middle finger, working until finger measures 3¼"/8.5cm.

Little finger
Sl 6 sts from back of hand to dpn, k these sts then pick up and k 2 sts at base of ring finger, k rem 6 sts—14 sts. Work until finger measures 2½"/6.5cm.
Dec rnd [K2tog] 7 times. K 1 rnd.
Dec rnd [K2tog] 3 times, k1—4 sts. Weave sts tog using Kitchener st.

Thumb
Place 15 sts of thumb onto 2 needles.
Rnd I K15, with 3rd needle, pick up and k 3 sts at base of thumb—18 sts. Cont in rnds until thumb measures 2¾"/7cm. Complete as for index finger.

LEFT GLOVE
Work as for right glove to thumb gore.
Rnd I K22, p1, M1, k1, M1, p1, k to end. Cont as for right glove to index finger.

Index finger
K17 and sl to contrast yarn strand, k16, cast on 2 sts for inner edge of finger, sl rem 23 sts to other end of yarn strand. Complete as for right glove.

FINISHING
Block gloves lightly. Fold picot hem to WS and sew in place. With disappearing marker, transfer embroidery motif to gloves foll photo for placement. Embroider stem in stem st, sew bugle beads and seed pearls in place.

Stitch key

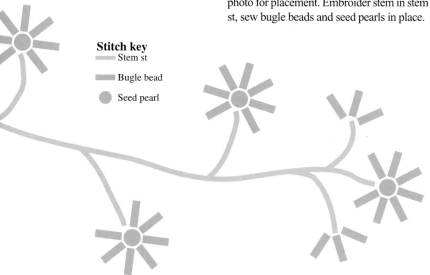

— Stem st

Bugle bead

● Seed pearl

CABLE TRELLIS MITTENS

Pattern play

For Experienced Knitters

Multiple cables cross to form a diamond on a purl-stitch background. The two side cables are joined together at the top with invisible Kitchener stitch weaving. Designed by Margaret Stove.

SIZES
One size fits Woman's size Small/Medium (7"-7½"/18cm-19cm).

MATERIALS
- 2 1¾oz/50g balls (each approx 121yd/110m) of Lane Borgosesia *Maratona*® (wool③) in #90424 pale blue
- One set (4) dpn size 5 (3.75mm) *or size to obtain gauge*
- Cable needle
- Stitch markers

GAUGE
21 sts and 36 rnds to 4"/10cm over St st using size 5 (3.75mm) needles.
Take time to check gauge.

STITCH GLOSSARY
3-st RPC
Sl 1 st to cn and hold to *back*, k2, p1 from cn.
3-st LPC
Sl 2 sts to cn and hold to *front*, p1, k2 from cn.
4-st RC
Sl 2 sts to cn and hold to *back*, k2, k2 from cn.
4-st LC
Sl 2 sts to cn and hold to *front*, k2, k2 from cn.

RIGHT MITTEN
Cast on 44 sts as foll: 14 sts on *Needle 1*; 16 sts on *Needle 2*; 14 sts on *Needle 3*. Join, taking care not to twist sts on needles. Work in k2, p2 rib for 20 rnds. Sl first 10 sts from *Needle 2* to end of *Needle 1* for back of hand and divide rem 20 sts onto 2 needles for palm of hand.

Foundation rnd K2, p2, sl next 2 sts to cn and hold to *back*, p2, p2 from cn, sl next 2 sts to cn and hold to *front*, k1, k2 from cn, sl next st to cn and hold to *back*, k2, k1 from cn, sl next 2 sts to cn and hold to *back*, k2, p2 from cn, p2, sl next 2 sts to cn and hold to *front*, p2, k2 from cn (end of back of hand), [p4, M1] 3 times, p8 (palm of hand in reverse St st)—47 sts.

Beg chart
Rnd 1 K2, p6, k8, p6, k2, p23. Cont to work in this way foll chart over first 24 sts and p last 23 sts through rnd 4.

Thumb gore
Rnd 5 Work 24 sts foll chart, pm, M1, p1, M1, pm, p22. Work 2 rnds even.
Inc rnd Work to first marker, sl marker, M1, p to 2nd marker, M1, sl marker, p to end. Rep inc rnd every 3rd rnd 5 times more—15 sts between markers. Work rnd 24.

Rnd 25 Work 24 sts foll chart, sl next 15 sts to contrast yarn strand for thumb, cast on 3 sts over these sts for other side of thumb, p to end—49 sts. Cont to work foll chart through rnd 51. Reposition sts beg at center of palm as foll: 13 sts on *Needle 1*; 24 sts on *Needle 2*; 12 sts on *Needle 3*. Use chart as a guide and foll instructions for shaping at top.

Top shaping
Rnd 52 P11, p2tog; p1, k2tog, k3, p4, k4, p4, k3, ssk, p1; p2tog, p10.
Rnd 53 P12; p1, k4, p4, 4-st LC, p4, k4, p1; p11.
Rnd 54 P10, p2tog; k2tog, k3, p4, k4, p4, k3, ssk; p2tog, p9.
Rnd 55 P11; [k4, p4] twice, k4; p10.
Rnd 56 P9, p2tog; [k4, p4] twice, k4; p2tog, p8.
Rnd 57 P10; 4-st LC, p4, k4, p4, 4-st LC; p9.
Rnd 58 P8, p2tog; [k4, p4] twice, k4; p2tog, p7.

Rnd 59 P9; k4, p4, 4-st LC, p4, k4; p8.

Rnd 60 P7, p2tog; k3, k2tog, p3, k4, p3, k2tog, k3; p2tog, p6.

Rnd 61 P6, p2tog; k4, p2, 3-st RPC, 3-st LPC, p2, k4; p2tog, p5.

Rnd 62 P5, p2tog; k3, ssk, p1, k2, p2, k2, p1, k2tog, k3; p2tog, p4.

Rnd 650 P4, p2tog; 4-st LC, p1, k2, p2, k2, p1, 4-st LC; p2tog, p3.

Rnd 64 P3, p2tog; k3, ssk, k2, p2, k2, k2tog, k3; p2tog, bind off 4 sts, p2tog, pass last bound-off st over p2tog, then k2tog first st of cable with last st of bind-off, k3. Place these 4 sts on a safety pin, bind off 5 sts, then k last st of bind-off tog with first st of cable, k3. Cont in St st on these 4 sts (working back and forth) for 3 rows more.

Next row (RS) Work 4-st LC. P 1 row. Sl these 4 sts and 4 sts on safety pin to 2 needles and weave tog at center top.

Thumb

Place 15 sts from thumb onto 2 needles.

Rnd 1 P15, with 3rd needle, pick up and p 3 sts at base of thumb—18 sts. P 16 rnds.

Dec rnd [P1, p2tog] 6 times. P 1 rnd.

Dec rnd [P2tog] 6 times. Cut yarn and draw through rem 6 sts. Fasten off.

LEFT MITTEN

Work as for right mitten to thumb gore.

Thumb gore

Rnd 5 Work 24 sts foll chart, p22, pm, M1, p1, M1, pm. Cont as for right mitten with thumb placement in reverse.

FINISHING

Block lightly. Sew sides of the cable along top of mitten at bound-off edge.

BACK OF HAND CHART

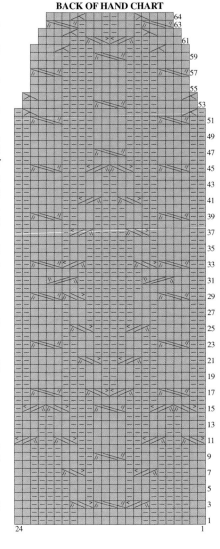

Stitch key

K on RS, p on WS

P on RS, k on WS

3-st RPC

3-st LPC

4-st RC

4-st LC

SSK

K2tog

BUTTONED RIB GLOVES

Invitation to elegance

For Intermediate Knitters

Knit in fine cashmere, these exquisite reversible elbow-length gloves are sure to become a traditional wardrobe staple. Buttons can be along the wrist or back of the hand. Designed by Mari Lynn Patrick.

SIZES

Instructions are written for Woman's size Small (7"/18cm). Changes for Medium (7½"/19cm) and Large (8"/20cm) are in parentheses. Shown in size Medium.

MATERIALS

■ 4 .88oz/25g balls (each approx 109yd/98m) of Grignasco/JCA *Cashmere* (cashmere②) in #582 grey
■ One pair size 2 (2.5mm) needles
■ 1 set (5) dpn size 2 (2.5mm) or *size to obtain gauge*
■ 22 ³⁄₈"/10mm buttons
■ Stitch markers

GAUGES

■ 36 sts and 40 rows to 4"/10cm over rib pat using size 2 (2.5mm) needles.
■ 28 sts and 40 rnds to 4"/10cm over St st using size 2 (2.5mm) needles.
Take time to check gauges.

RIGHT GLOVE

With size 2 (2.5mm) straight needles, cast on 65 (70, 75) sts.

Row 1 (RS) K2, p2, [k2, p3] 11 (12, 13) times, k2, p2, k2. Cont in rib as established for 1 row.

Next (buttonhole) row (RS) K2, p2tog, yo (for buttonhole), [k2, p3] 11 (12, 13) times, k2, p2, k2. Rep buttonhole row every 8th row 10 times more, AT SAME TIME, work as foll when piece measures 3"/7.5cm from beg:

Dec row (RS) K2, p2, [k2, p2tog, p1] twice, [k2, p3] 7 (8, 9) times, [k2, p2tog, p1] twice, k2, p2, k2. Work decs in p ribs every 1"/2.5cm or 10th row twice more ONLY working 2nd dec row in 3rd & 4th and 8th & 9th (9 & 10th, 10th & 11th) p ribs and 3rd dec row in 5th & 6th & 7th (7th & 8th, 7th & 8th & 9th) p ribs. Work even in k2, p2 rib on rem 54 (58, 62) sts until piece measures 8"/20.5cm from beg. Work even for 3 more rows after last (11th) buttonhole.

Next (joining) rnd (RS) With dpn, sl first 16 (17, 19) sts to *Needle 1*, 16 (18, 18) sts to *Needle 2*, 16 (17, 19) sts to *Needle 3*, 6 sts to *Needle 4*. Place last 6 sts (*Needle 4*) behind *Needle 1* and [k1 st tog from *Needle 1* with 1 st from *Needle 4*] 6 times for overlap; then k1 st in each rem st around—there are 16 (17, 19) sts on *Needle 1*; 16 (18, 18) sts on *Needle 2*; 16 (17, 19) sts on *Needle 3*, for a total of 48 (52, 56) sts. Mark end of rnd and sl marker every rnd. Cont in rnds of St st as foll:

Thumb gore

Next rnd K sts of *Needles 1 and 2*, k3 (3, 4) sts of *Needle 3*—13 (14, 15) sts rem on *Needle 3*, pm, inc 1 st in each of next 2 sts (to inc, k1 into front and back of each st), pm, work to end of rnd. *Work 2 rnds even.

Next rnd K to marker, inc 1 st in next st, k to 1 st before next marker inc 1 st in next st, k to end*. Rep between *'s 6 times more—18 sts between markers for thumb. K 1 rnd on all sts.

Next rnd K to 18 marked thumb sts, sl these sts to a contrast yarn strand and cast on 2 sts over the thumb sts—48 (52, 56) sts. Work even until hand measures 4 (4½, 5)"/10 (11.5, 12.5)cm above rib or desired length to base of fingers.

Index finger

Work 16 (17, 19) sts *Needle 1*, 13 (15, 15) sts *Needle 2*, with separate needle, work next 14 (14, 16) sts, sl all rem 34 (38, 40) sts to contrast yarn strand to be worked later. Cast on 2 sts at end of 14 (14, 16) sts on needle and dividing these 16 (16, 18) sts onto 3 needles, work in rnds of St st until finger measures 2¾ (3, 3¼)"/7 (7.5, 8)cm OR ¼"/.5cm less than desired length. (See sizing on page 12 for an accurate fit).
Dec rnd [K2tog, k2] 4 times, [k2tog] 0 (0, 1) time—12 (12, 13) sts. K 1 rnd.
Dec rnd K0 (0, 3), [k2tog, k1 (1, 0)] 4 (4, 5) times—8 sts. Weave sts tog using Kitchener st.

Middle finger

Sl 6 (7, 7) sts from back of hand to dpn, k these sts then pick up and k 3 sts at base of index finger, k6 (7, 7) sts from palm of hand, cast on 3 (2, 2) sts at end—18 (19, 19) sts. Work in rnds of St st until finger measures 3¼ (3½, 3¾)"/8.5 (9, 9.5)cm.
Dec rnd K2 (1, 1), [k2tog, k2] 4 times, [k2tog] 0 (1, 1) time—14 sts. K 1 rnd.
Dec rnd K1, [k2tog, k1] 4 times, k1—10 sts. Weave sts tog.

Ring finger

Sl 6 (6, 7) sts from back of hand to dpn, k these sts then pick up and k 2 sts at base of middle finger, k6 (6, 7) sts from palm of hand, cast on 2 sts at end—16 (16, 18) sts. Work until finger measures 3 (3¼, 3½)"/7.5 (8, 9)cm. Complete as for index finger.

Little finger

Sl 5 (6, 6) sts from back of hand to dpn, k these sts then pick up and k 3 (2, 2) st at base of ring finger, k5 (6, 6) sts from palm of hand—13 (14, 14) sts. Work in rnds of St st until finger measures 2¼ (2½, 2¾)"/6 (6.5, 7)cm.
Dec rnd K1 (2, 2), [k2tog, k2] 3 times—10 (11, 11) sts. K 1 rnd.
Dec rnd K2, [k2tog, k1] 2 (3, 3) times, k2 (0, 0)—8 sts. Weave sts tog.

Thumb

Place 18 sts of thumb onto 2 needles.
Rnd 1 K18, with 3rd needle, pick up and k 8 sts at base of thumb—26 sts. K 1 rnd.
Next rnd K18, on 3rd needle, k2, ssk, k2tog, k2—24 sts.
Next rnd K18; k1, ssk, k2tog, k1.
Next rnd K18; ssk, k2tog—20 sts. Divide sts onto 3 needles and work in rnds of St st until thumb measures 2¾"/7cm.
Dec rnd [K2, k2tog] 5 times—15 sts. K 1 rnd.
Dec rnd [K2tog, k1] 5 times—10 sts. Weave sts tog.

LEFT GLOVE

Work as for right glove through joining rnd—48 (52, 56) sts.

Beg thumb

Next rnd K14 (15, 16) sts of *Needle 1*, pm, inc 1 st in each of next 2 sts, pm, work to end. Cont as for right glove with fingers in reverse.

FINISHING

Block pieces lightly. Sew on buttons.

GAUNTLET MITTENS

Gothically speaking

Striking mittens are adorned with color, slipped stitchwork and style to spare. Woven I-cords at the wrist add to the drama. Designed by Deborah Newton.

SIZES

One size fits Medium/Large (7½"-8"/ 19cm-20cm).

MATERIALS

■ 1 1¾oz/50g skein (each approx 137yd/ 126m) of Classic Elite *Waterspun* (wool④) each in #5026 dk purple (MC), #5085 pumpkin (A), #5097 moss (B), #5005 hot pink (C), #5075 grey (D), #5068 dk orange (E), #5039 camel (F) and #5032 magenta (G).

■ One set (5) dpn size 7 (4.5mm) *or size to obtain gauge*

GAUGES

■ 17 sts and 32 rnds to 4"/10cm over slip stitch pat using size 7 (4.5mm) needles

■ 21 sts and 24 rnds to 4"/10cm over St st and pat foll chart using size 7 (4.5mm) needles. *Take time to check gauges.*

Note To avoid long stands at inside of glove when foll chart, twist yarns tog every other st.

SLIP STITCH PATTERN

(multiple of 4 sts)

Rnds 1 and 2 With MC, knit.

Rnd 3 With MC, *k3, k1 wrapping yarn around needle twice; rep from * around.

Rnd 4 With A, *k1, insert needle into next st 2 rows below and draw up a long lp, k next st and pass lp over st just knitted, k1, sl 1 wyib dropping extra wrap; rep from * around.

Rnd 5 With A, *k3, sl 1 wyib; rep from * around.

Rnd 6 With A, knit.

Rnd 7 With A, *k3, k1 wrapping yarn around needle twice; rep from * around.

Rep rnds 4-7 for sl st pat working 4 rnds with B, 4 rnds C, 4 rnds D, 4 rnds E, 4 rnds F, 4 rnds G, then 4 rnds A.

RIGHT MITTEN

Cuff

With MC, cast on 48 sts over 4 needles having 12 sts on each needle. Join, taking care not to twist sts on needles. Mark end of rnd and sl marker every rnd. Work sl st pat until 2nd set of A rnds are completed. With MC, work rnds 4, 5 and 6. K 1 more rnd with MC. With G, k 1 rnd and p 1 rnd firmly.

Next rnd With G, [k2tog, k1] 16 times— 32 sts. K 2 rnds.

Next (eyelet) rnd With MC, *k2tog, yo, k1, k2tog, yo, k2; rep from * 3 times more, end k2tog, yo, k2 (9 eyelets). K 1 rnd.

Next (inc) rnd *[K3, inc 1 st in next st] twice, k2, [k1, inc 1 st in next st] 3 times; rep from * once—42 sts.

Hand

Rnd 1 Work rnd 1 of hand chart as foll: work 6-st rep 7 times. Cont to foll chart through rnd 15.

Thumb opening

Next rnd K2 sts, with scrap yarn k7, sl 7 sts (in scrap yarn) back to LH needle and k these sts then cont in pat to end. Cont to foll chart until 33 rnds have been worked in chart pat, end with rnd 15.

Top shaping

K 1 rnd with MC.

Dec rnd With A, work as foll: *Needle 1* Ssk, k to end; *Needle 2* K to last 2 sts, k2tog; *Needle 3* Ssk, k to end; *Needle 4* K to last 2 sts, k2tog (4 sts dec)—38 sts.

Next rnd With A, knit. Rep last 2 rnds, working stripes as foll: 1 rnd MC, 1 rnd B, 2 rnds G, 2 rnds C, 1 rnd G, 1 rnd D, 2 rnds MC, 2 rnds A, 4 rnds MC—6 sts rem. [K3tog] twice. Cut yarn and draw through rem 2 sts. Fasten off.

Thumb

Carefully remove scarp yarn. Sl 1 dpn through 7 lps at bottom, sl 2 more dpn through 6 upside-down lps at top of opening. Pick up a lp at each side of thumb and sl to last 2 needles, pick up a lp at inner corner and sl to first needle—16 sts. Join G and working in rnds, k 6 rnds. K 2 rnds C, 1 rnd MC, 1 rnd D, 3 rnds MC. Dec as for mitten top until 4 sts rem. K2tog twice.

Cut yarn and draw through rem sts. Fasten off.

LEFT MITTEN

Work as for right mitten to thumb opening.
Next rnd K12, k7 sts onto scrap yarn and complete as for right mitten.

FINISHING

Block pieces lightly.

I-Cord trim

(make 2 each C and D)
With 2 dpn, cast on 3 sts. *Slide sts to other end of needle. Bring yarn around from back and k3. Rep from * until cord is 14"/36cm long. Bind off. Weave cords through eyelet rnd as in photo. Wind A several times around cords to secure.

HAND CHART

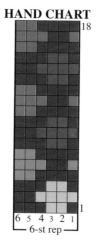

6 5 4 3 2 1
6-st rep

Color key

■ Dk purple (MC)

■ Pumpkin (A)

■ Moss (B)

■ Hot pink (C)

■ Grey (D)

■ Dk orange (E)

□ Camel (F)

CABLE-FRONT GLOVES

Fancy fingerwork

A combination of easy right-twist and left-twist patterns make up these guernsey-inspired gloves designed by Norah Gaughan. A plain Stockinette-stitch palm helps them retain their grip.

SIZES

One size fits Woman's size X-Small to Small (6½"-7"/17cm-18cm).

MATERIALS

■ 2 1¾oz/50g balls (each approx 110yd/101m) of Reynolds/JCA *Paterna* (wool④) in #841 rose

■ 1 set (4) dpn size 5 (3.75mm) *or size to obtain gauge*

■ Stitch holders

GAUGE

20 sts and 28 rnds to 4"/10cm over St st using size 5 (3.75mm) needles.

Take time to check gauge.

STITCH GLOSSARY

RT

Pass in front of first st and k 2nd st, then k first st and let both sts fall from needle.

LT

Pass in back of first st and k 2nd st tbl, then k first st and let both sts fall from needle.

LEFT GLOVE

Cast on 39 sts. Divide sts onto 3 needles as foll: 20 sts on *Needle 1*; 10 sts on *Needle 2*; 9 sts on *Needle 3*. Join, taking care not to twist sts on needles. Mark end of rnd and sl marker every rnd. P 1 rnd, k 1 rnd.

Rnd 1 Work rnd 1 of chart over first 20 sts; p1, [k1 tbl, p1] 9 times. Cont in pat as established through rnd 14 of chart.

Rnd 15 Work rnd 15 of chart over first 20 sts; p1, k to last st of rnd, p1. Cont in pat as established through rnd 21 of chart.

Thumb gore

Next rnd Work to last 3 sts of rnd, M1, k2, M1, p1. Work 1 rnd even.

Next rnd Work to last 5 sts of rnd, M1, k4, M1, p1. Work 1 rnd even.

Next rnd Work to last 7 sts of rnd, M1, k6, M1, p1. Work 1 rnd even.

Next rnd Work to last 9 sts of rnd, M1, k8, M1, p1. Work 1 rnd even.

Next rnd Work to last 11 sts of rnd, sl next 10 sts to a holder and cast on 4 sts for inside of thumb, p1—41 sts. Work even in established pat through rnd 41 of chart. Sl first 5 sts to *Needle 1*; sl next 15 sts to one holder; sl foll 15 sts to 2nd holder; sl rem 6 sts to *Needle 3*.

Note Cont foll chart for front of each finger.

Index finger

Foll chart for 5 sts of *Needle 1*; cast on 4 sts on *Needle 2*; k5, p1 for *Needle 3*—15 sts.

Next rnd Work 5 sts of chart, p1, k8, p1. Cont to work in rnds in this way until chart for index finger is completed.

Dec rnd K1, [k2tog] 7 times. Cut yarn and draw through rem 8 sts. Fasten off.

Middle finger

Pick up and k 3 sts at base of index finger for *Needle 1*, from front holder, work 5 sts of chart for *Needle 2*, cast on 3 sts on *Needle 3*, then k5 from back holder—16 sts. Redistribute sts evenly on 3 needles.

Next rnd K2, p1, work 5 sts of chart, k8. Cont in this way until chart for middle finger is completed.

Dec rnd [K2tog] 8 times. Cut yarn and draw through rem 8 sts. Fasten off.

Ring finger

Pick up and k 3 sts at base of middle finger, from front holder work 5 sts of chart, cast on 3 sts, then k5 from back holder—16 sts.

Next rnd K3, work 5 sts of chart, p1, k7. Cont to end of chart for ring finger and complete as for middle finger.

Little finger
Pick up and k 4 sts at base of ring finger, from front holder work 5 sts of chart, from back holder p1, k4—14 sts.

Next rnd K3, p1, work 5 sts of chart, p1, k4. Work as for other fingers until chart is completed.

Dec rnd [K2tog] 7 times. Cut yarn and draw through rem 7 sts. Fasten off.

Thumb
Pick up and k 5 sts at base of thumb, place 10 sts from holder onto 2 needles and k these sts—15 sts. Cont in rnds of St st until thumb measures 2½"/6.5cm.

Dec rnd K1, [k2tog] 7 times. Cut yarn and draw through rem 7 sts. Fasten off.

RIGHT GLOVE
Work to correspond to left glove reversing placement of thumb gusset and position of other fingers.

FINISHING
Block gloves lightly, taking care not to flatten out.

Stitch key

☐ K

⊟ P

▱ RT

▨ LT

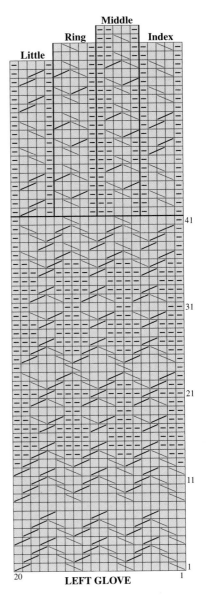

Little   Ring   Middle   Index

41

31

21

11

20   **LEFT GLOVE**   1

For Experienced Knitters

Magnificent color patterning, flared gauntlet styling, and scalloped cuffs give these gloves striking attitude. The pattern is adopted from Inca textiles circa 1000-1450 A.D. Designed by Nadia Severns.

SIZES
One size fits Woman's Small/Medium (7"-7½"/18cm-19cm).

MATERIALS
■ 2 1¾oz/50g skeins (each approx 124yd/115m) of Rowan/Westminster Fibers *Designer DK* (wool②) in #62 black (MC)
■ 1 .88oz/25g skein (each approx 108yd/100m) of Rowan Westminster Fibers *Lightweight DK* (wool②) each in #126 purple (A), #96 magenta (B), #013 yellow (C), #124 green (D), #510 orange (E) and #057 blue (F).
■ One set (5) dpn each sizes 3 and 4 (3 and 3.5mm) or *size to obtain gauge*
■ One pair size 6 (4mm) straight needles
■ Stitch markers

GAUGE
26 sts and 32 rnds to 4"/10cm over St st and chart pat using size 4 (3.5mm) needles.
Take time to check gauge.

Note To avoid long strands at inside of gloves, twist yarns tog every other st throughout hand and every st while working fingers.

LEFT GLOVE
With size 6 (4mm) straight needles, cast on with 2 colors as foll: using double cast-on method (see page 15), and using long strands of colors MC (held over thumb) and A (held over index finger), cast on 90 sts. Be sure not to pull sts tightly when casting on. Divide sts onto 4 size 4 (3.5mm) needles as foll: 18 sts on *Needle 1*; 27 sts on *Needle 2*; 18 sts on *Needle 3*, 27 sts on *Needle 4*. Join, taking care not to twist sts on needle. Mark end of rnd and sl marker every rnd.

Scallop edge
Rnd 1 With A, purl.
Rnd 2 With B, *k2tog tbl, k2, yo, k1, yo, k2, k2tog; rep from * around.
Rnd 3 With B, *k2tog tbl, k2, yo, sl 1, yo, k2, k2tog; rep from * around.
Rnds 4 and 5 With C, rep rnds 2 and 3.
Rnd 6 With MC, k1, *k7 C, k2 MC; rep from *, end k7 C, k1 MC.

Gauntlet
Redistribute sts on size 3 (3mm) dpn as foll: 22 sts on *Needle 1*, 23 sts on *Needle 2*; 22 sts on *Needle 3*; 23 sts on *Needle 4*.

Beg Gauntlet chart
Work rnds 1-6 of chart
Rnd 7 Ssk, work to last 2 sts of *Needle 2*, k2tog; at beg of *Needle 3*, ssk, work to last 2 sts of *Needle 4*, k2tog (4 sts dec). Cont in this way to dec 4 sts every 6th rnd foll chart, 5 times more.
Rnd 39 Dec 12 sts evenly spaced around—54 sts.
Rnd 40 Dec 4 sts as on rnd 7—50 sts. Work to end of chart (rnd 46).

Hand
Notes 1) To inc for thumb gore, lift thread between 2 sts and k tbl (M1). **2)** For left glove, palm is worked on *Needles 1 and 2*, back is worked on *Needles 3 and 4* (and in reverse for the right glove).
Work pat foll hand chart through rnd 5.
Rnd 6 Work 22 sts, pm, k1, pm, work to end. See on chart that the st between markers will be omitted and replaced with sts shown on thumb chart.

Thumb gore
Rnd 7 Work to marker, with D, M1, k1,

M1 (rnd 7 of thumb gore chart), work to end. Replacing thumb pat sts as indicated, work in pat foll charts for 1 rnd.

Rnd 9 Work to marker, M1, k3, M1, work to end. Cont in this way to foll charts and inc 1 st each side and foll thumb chart through rnd 24.

Next rnd Work to thumb gore, sl 19 sts of thumb to contrast yarn strand and cast on 1 st for inside edge of thumb—50 sts. Work even through rnd 31 of hand chart. Sl last 5 sts of *Needle 4* (back) and first 6 sts of *Needle 1* (palm) to contrast yarn strand for little finger (to be worked later).

Next rnd With MC, cast on 3 sts onto *Needle 1* for inner edge of finger (to join other 3 fingers) and work 1 rnd even on 42 sts.

Ring finger

Note fingers will be divided on 3 needles.

Next rnd With MC, k6 sts *Needle 1*, k3 sts from *Needle 2*, cast on 3 sts for inner edge of finger, sl next 27 sts to contrast yarn strand, k last 6 sts of *Needle 4*—18 sts. K 1 rnd with MC. Centering chart on finger, work in pat foll ring finger chart through rnd 19. K 1 rnd with MC.

Dec rnd [K1, k2tog] 6 times—12 sts.

Dec rnd [K2tog] 6 times. Cut yarn and draw through rem sts. Fasten off.

Middle finger

With MC, beg at center of 3 cast-on sts of ring finger, pick up and k 3 sts, sl 6 sts from palm to dpn and k these sts, cast on 3 sts, work 6 sts from back, pick up and k 2 sts at end—20 sts.

Next rnd With MC k2, k2tog, k to last 3 sts, ssk, k1—18 sts. Work as for ring finger foll chart through rnd 24. Complete as for ring finger.

Index finger

With MC, beg at center of 3 cast-on sts of middle finger pick up and k 3 sts, sl rem 15 sts to dpn and k these sts, pick up and k 2 sts at end—20 sts.

Next rnd With MC, k2, k2tog, k to last 3 sts, ssk, k1—18 sts. Work index finger chart and complete as for ring finger.

Little finger

With MC, beg at center of 3 cast-on sts of ring finger, pick up and k 3 sts, work rem 11 sts, pick up and k 2 sts at end—16 sts.

Next rnd With MC, k1, k2tog, k to last 3 sts, ssk, k2—14 sts. Work foll chart through rnd 13.

Dec rnd [K1, k2tog] 4 times k2—10 sts.

Dec rnd [K2tog] 5 times. Cut yarn and draw through rem sts. Fasten off.

Thumb

Place 19 sts of thumb onto 2 needles.

Rnd 1 Foll thumb chart, k19, pick up and work in pat 5 sts—24 sts.

Rnd 1 Work to last 5 sts, ssk with B, k3 MC, k2tog with B—22 sts.

Rnd 2 Work even.

Rnd 3 Dec 2 sts at inner edge of thumb to foll color pat—20 sts. Cont in pat foll chart through rnd 12. Cont with MC only.

Dec rnd [K5, k2tog] twice, k4, k2tog—17 sts. Work 1 rnd even.

Dec rnd [K4, k2tog] twice, k3, k2tog—14 sts. Work 1 rnd even.

Dec rnd [K3, k2tog] twice, k2, k2tog—11 sts. Work 1 rnd even.

Dec rnd [K2, k2tog] twice, k1, k2tog. Cut yarn and draw through rem 8 sts. Fasten off.

RIGHT GLOVE

Work as for left glove foll chart for placement of palm and back of hand sts. Note that thumb gore starts at beg of *Needle 3* and all fingers will be worked in reverse.

FINISHING

Block lightly.

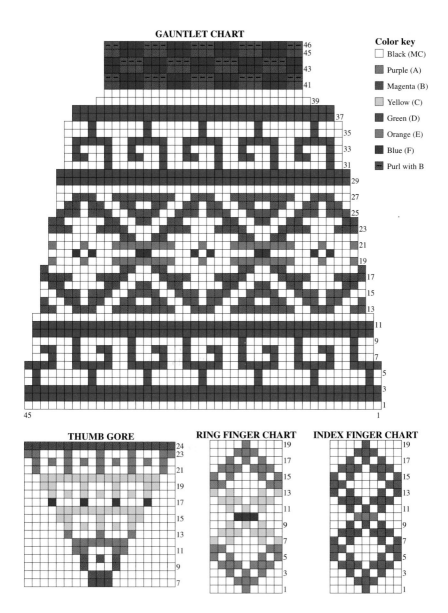

GAUNTLET CHART

Color key

☐ Black (MC)
⬛ Purple (A)
⬛ Magenta (B)
☐ Yellow (C)
⬛ Green (D)
⬛ Orange (E)
⬛ Blue (F)
〰 Purl with B

THUMB GORE

RING FINGER CHART

INDEX FINGER CHART

63

HAND CHART

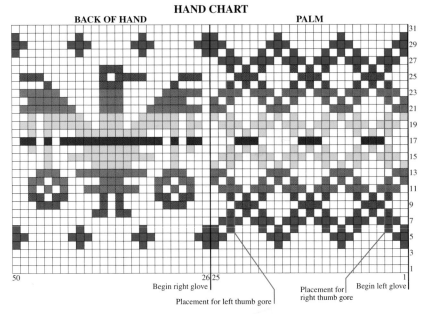

BACK OF HAND   PALM

50   26|25   1

Begin right glove

Placement for left thumb gore

Placement for right thumb gore

Begin left glove

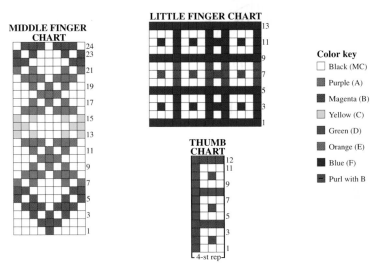

MIDDLE FINGER CHART

LITTLE FINGER CHART

THUMB CHART

4-st rep

Color key

☐ Black (MC)

■ Purple (A)

■ Magenta (B)

☐ Yellow (C)

■ Green (D)

■ Orange (E)

■ Blue (F)

▬ Purl with B

FELTED MITTENS
Stripe it rich

For Intermediate Knitters

For winter nights and snowball fights, these mittens are your best bet for staying warm and cozy. Light felting after knitting provides interesting texture and extra warmth. Designed by Linda Niemeyer.

SIZES
Instructions are written for Adult's size Medium (7½"/19cm). Change for Large (8"/20.5cm) and X-Large (8½"/21.5cm) are in parentheses. Shown in size Medium.

MATERIALS
■ 2 2oz/60g skeins (each approx 120yd/108m) of Blue Sky Alpacas *Alpaca* (alpaca②) in #003 dk tan (MC)
■ 1 skein in #004 lt tan (CC)
■ 1 set (4) dpn size 11 (8mm) *or size to obtain gauge*
■ Stitch holders

GAUGE
14 sts and 18 rnds to 4"/10cm over St st (before felting) using double strand of yarn and size 11 (8mm) needles.
Take time to check gauge.

Notes 1) Knitted fabric is very loose knit and the felting process will give the solid appearance pictured here. **2)** Work with double strand of yarn throughout.

RIGHT MITTEN
With double strand of CC, cast on 24 (24, 28) sts. Divide sts onto 3 needles. Join, taking care not to twist sts on needles. Mark end of rnd and sl marker every rnd.

Rnd 1 *K2, p2; rep from * around. Change to MC and cont in rib for 12 (12, 14) rnds more. Cont in St st as foll:
Next rnd With MC, k12 (12, 14), inc 0 (1, 1) by M1, k12 (12, 14), inc 0 (1, 1)—24 (26, 30) sts. Work even for 4 (4, 5) rnds.

Thumb gore
Rnd 1 M1, k1, M1, k to end.
Rnd 2 Knit.
Rnd 3 M1, k3, M1, k to end.
Rnd 4 Change to CC and knit.
Rnd 5 M1, k5, M1, k to end.
Rnd 6 Knit.
Rnd 7 M1, k7, M1, k to end.
Rnd 8 and 9 Knit.
For X-Large size only:
Rnd 10 M1, k9, M1, k to end.
Rnd 11 Knit.

Hand
Next rnd (all sizes) Change to MC, k1, place 7 (7, 9) sts on a holder for thumb, cast on 3 sts over these sts and k to end—28 (30, 34) sts. Work 7 (8, 10) rnds even with MC. Change to CC and work 5 (6, 7) rnds. Change to MC and cont with MC to end of mitten.

Top shaping
Dec rnd *Ssk, k10 (11, 13), k2tog; rep from * once. K 2 rnds.
Dec rnd *Ssk, k8 (9, 11), k2tog; rep from * once. K 2 rnds.
Dec rnd *Ssk, k1, ssk, k0 (1, 3), k2tog, k1, k2tog; rep from * once. K 1 rnd.
Dec rnd *[Ssk] 1 (1, 2) times, k2 (3, 1), k2tog 1 (1, 2) times; rep from * once—8 (10, 10) sts.
Dec rnd [K2tog] 4, (5, 5) times. Cut yarn and draw through rem 4 sts. Fasten off.

Thumb

Place 7 (7, 9) sts of thumb onto 2 needles.
Rnd I With MC, k7 (7, 9), pick up and k 5 sts at base of thumb—12 (12, 14) sts. K 6 (7, 8) rnds.
Dec rnd K0 (0, 2), [k2tog, k1] 4 times—8 (8, 10) sts. K 1 rnd.
Dec rnd [K2tog] 4 (4, 5) times. Cut yarn and draw through rem 4 (4, 5) sts. Fasten off.

LEFT MITTEN

Work as for right mitten to thumb gore.

Thumb gore

Rnd I K23 (25, 29), M1, k1, M1. Cont as for right mitten reversing thumb.

FINISHING

Fill basin with warm water and a mild soap and soak mittens. Agitate for 3 minutes. Rinse with cold water. Refill with warm water and repeat. Mittens may be shaped to fit hand measurement at this point. Roll in a towel, lay flat and shape to dry.

These mittens follow the natural wave of a classic chevron pattern stitch beginning at the fingertips and working down to the curved cuffs. For the thumb, stitches are picked up around an opening and worked in the opposite direction. Designed by Rosemary Drysdale.

SIZES

One size fits Woman's X-Small (6½"/17cm).

MATERIALS

■ 1 1¾oz/50g ball (each approx 146yd/136m) of Filatura Di Crosa/Stacy Charles *Sympathie Tweed* (wool/mohair/acrylic/viscose④) in #165 rust tweed
■ Size 4 (3.5mm) straight needles *or size to obtain gauge*
■ 1 set (4) dpn size 4 (3.5mm)

GAUGE

29 sts and 30 rows to 4"/10cm over chevron pat st using size 4 (3.5mm) needles.
Take time to check gauge.

Note Mittens are knit straight beg at top edge and ending at cuff. The natural curve of the pattern stitch forms the mitten top.

LEFT MITTEN

Cast on 48 sts.
Rows 1 and 3 Knit.
Row 2 Purl.
Row 4 (WS) [Yo, p1] 4 times, [k2tog] 8 times, [yo, p1] 8 times, [k2tog] 8 times, [yo, p1] 4 times.

Rep rows 1-4 for chevron pat 7 times more then work row 1 once more.

Thumb opening

Next row P16, sl next 8 sts to a contrast yarn strand for thumb, turn work to the RS and cast on 8 sts using 2-needle method, turn to WS and p rem 24 sts. Cont in pat st on 48 sts until a total of 15 pat reps are completed. K 3 rows. Bind off knitwise.

Thumb

From RS with dpn, on the palm side of mitten, pick up and k 8 sts in cast-on sts, pick up and k 4 sts along side edge of opening, sl 8 sts from holder to dpn, pick up and k 4 sts along other side of opening—24 sts. Do not join. Working back and forth in rows, work rows 2 and 3 of pat.
Row 4 (WS) [Yo, p1] 4 times, [k2tog] 8 times, [yo, p1] 4 times. Rep rows 1-4 twice then work rows 1-3 once.
Next row P4, [k2tog] 8 times, p4—16 sts. K 1 row, p 1 row, k 1 row.
Next row [K2tog] 8 times while binding off at same time.

RIGHT MITTEN

Work as for left mitten to thumb opening.

Thumb opening

Next row P24, sl next 8 sts to a contrast yarn strand for thumb, turn work to RS and cast on 8 sts using 2-needle method, turn to WS and p rem 16 sts. Complete as for left mitten.

FINISHING

Block lightly. Sew side and thumb seam.

HOUNDSTOOTH MITTENS

Tailor made

Tweedy mohair mittens in a classic houndstooth check pattern provide a lightweight layer of warmth. Easy to knit on two needles, the fuzzy texture renders seams virtually invisible. Designed by Jean Guirguis.

SIZES

One size fits Woman's Small/Medium (7"-7½"/18cm-19cm).

MATERIALS

■ 1 3½oz/100g skein (each approx 190yd/175m) of Colinette/Unique Kolours *Mohair* (mohair/wool/nylon⑤) each in #70 Raphael (A) and #UK01 soft sienna (B)
■ 1 pair each sizes 8 and 9 (5 and 5.5mm) straights needles *or size to obtain gauge*
■ Stitch holders

GAUGE

16 sts and 18 rows to 4"/10cm over St st foll chart using larger needles.
Take time to check gauge.

LEFT MITTEN

With smaller needles and A, cast on 32 sts. Work in k1, p1 rib for 3"/7.5cm. Change to larger needles. Cont in St st as foll:

Beg houndstooth chart
Row 1 (RS) Work 4-st rep 8 times.
Next row Work chart row 2.
Inc row Inc 1 st each end of row, working incs into chart pat. Work 1 row even. Rep inc row—36 sts. Work even in pat foll chart for 3 rows more. Cut yarn.

Thumb

From RS, sl first 14 sts to a holder, work 8 sts in chart, sl rem 14 sts to a holder.

Next row (WS) Inc 1 st in first st, p6, inc 1 st in last st—10 sts. Work chart pat for 6 rows more.
Dec row [K2tog] 5 times. P 1 row. Cut yarn and draw through rem 5 sts. Fasten off. Sew thumb seam.

Hand

Rejoin yarn to sts from first holder, pick up and k 4 sts at base of thumb, k14 from 2nd holder—32 sts. Cont in chart pat until mitten measures 8"/20.5cm from beg, end with a WS row.

Top shaping

Next row (RS) K2tog tbl, k12, [k2tog] twice, k12, k2tog—28 sts. P 1 row.
Next row K2tog tbl, k10, [k2tog] twice, k10, k2tog—24 sts. P 1 row.
Next row K2tog tbl, k8, [k2tog] twice, k8, k2tog—20 sts. P 1 row.
Next row K2tog tbl, k6, [k2tog] twice, k6, k2tog—16 sts. Bind off.

RIGHT MITTEN

Work as for left mitten (mittens are reversible).

FINISHING

Block mittens lightly. Sew bound-off sts tog at top of hand. Sew side seam.

HOUNDSTOOTH CHART

4

1

└4-st rep┘

Color key
■ Raphael (A)
■ Soft sienna (B)

Show your wild side

For Experienced Knitters

Zebra-patterned gloves are trimmed with stretch faux-fur cuffs. The under cuff is worked in k1,p1 rib for a snug fit. Designed by Gitta Schrade.

SIZES
One size fits Woman's X-Small 6½"/17cm.

MATERIALS
■ 1 1¾oz/50g ball (each approx 140yd/130m) of Schoeller Esslinger/Skacel Collection *Merino Soft* (wool③) each in #2 black (A) and #1 white (B)
■ 1 1¾oz/50g ball (each approx 48yd/45m) of Mondial/Skacel Collection *Fur* (wool/acrylic/polyester⑥) in #89 black (C)
■ One set (4) dpn size 4 (3.5mm) *or size to obtain gauge*
■ One pair size 8 (5mm) straight needles
■ Stitch holders and markers

GAUGE
28 sts and 28 rnds to 4"/10cm over St st and pat foll chart using size 4 (3.5mm) needles. *Take time to check gauge.*

Notes 1) Fur cuff is knit after working glove and sewn on top of rib cuff. **2)** To avoid long strands at inside of gloves, twist yarns tog every other st throughout hand and every st while working fingers.

LEFT GLOVE
With dpn and A, cast on 48 sts. Divide sts onto 3 needles. Join, taking care not to twist sts on needles. Mark end of rnd and sl marker every rnd. Work in k1, p1 rib for 3"/7.5cm.
Beg hand chart
Rnd 1 Rep sts 1-24 twice. Cont to foll chart in this way through rnd 6.

Rnd 7 Work 46 sts, pm, work last 2 sts. Note on chart that the st after marker will be omitted when foll left thumb chart.
Thumb gore
Rnd 8 Work to marker, foll left thumb chart rnd 8, M1, k1, M1, work last st of hand chart. Replacing thumb pat sts as indicated, work in pat foll charts for 1 rnd.
Rnd 10 Work to marker, M1, k3, M1, work last st of hand chart. Cont in this way to foll charts and inc 1 st by M1 st each side foll thumb chart 4 times more.
Rnds 19 and 21 Work even foll charts.
Rnd 22 Work to marker, sl last 14 sts to contrast yarn strand for thumb and cast on 2 sts for inside edge of thumb—48 sts. Work even foll hand chart through rnd 32. This is the length of hand to base of index fingers. Fingers will cont to foll chart for the next 5 rnds then use chart only as a guide for the length of the fingers.
Little finger
Rnd 33 Work 19 sts and sl these sts to first holder (back of hand), work 10 sts, then sl rem 19 sts to 2nd holder (palm of hand), cast on 3 sts at end for inner edge of finger—13 sts. Join and work in rnds until finger measures 2¼"/6cm OR ¼"/.5cm less than desired length (see sizing on page 12 for an accurate fit).
Dec rnd [K2, k2tog] 3 times, k1.
Dec rnd [K2tog] 5 times. Cut yarn and draw through rem 5 sts. Fasten off.
Ring finger
Sl 6 sts from first holder to dpn and k these sts, pick up and k 3 sts at base of little finger, k6 sts from 2nd holder, cast on 2 sts at end—17 sts. Work in rnds until finger measures 3"/7.5cm.

Dec rnd [K2, k2tog] 4 times, k1.

Dec rnd K1, [k2tog] 6 times. Cut yarn and draw through rem 7 sts. Fasten off.

Middle finger

Work as for ring finger until finger measures 3¼"/8.5cm. Complete as for ring finger.

Index finger

Work 7 sts from first holder, pick up and k 3 sts at base of middle finger, work 7 sts from 2nd holder—17 sts. Work in rnds until finger measures 2¾"/7cm. Complete as for ring finger.

Thumb

Place 14 sts of thumb onto 2 needles.

Rnd 1 Foll thumb chart, k14, pick up and work in pat on 3 sts at base of thumb—17 sts. Work in rnds until thumb measures 2½"/6.5cm. Complete as for ring finger.

RIGHT GLOVE

Work as for left glove through rnd 6 of chart.

Rnd 7 Work 25 sts, pm, work to end. Cont as for left glove foll right thumb chart and sl 14 sts (1 st before marker) to contrast yarn strand for thumb. Work as for left glove to base of fingers.

Little finger

Rnd 23 Work 5 sts, sl 19 sts to first holder, sl 19 sts to 2nd holder, cast on 3 sts at inner edge of finger and work rem 5 sts—13 sts. Work fingers as for left glove.

FINISHING

Fur cuff

With size 8 (5mm) straight needles and C, cast on 8 sts (for width of cuff). Work in reverse St st until cuff fits around rib band of glove (stretching slightly). Bind off. Sew cuff seam. Sew cuff over rib band stretching slightly. Block gloves lightly.

LEFT THUMB CHART

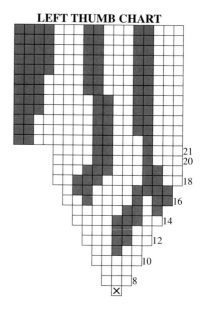

RIGHT THUMB CHART

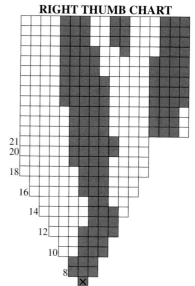

HAND CHART

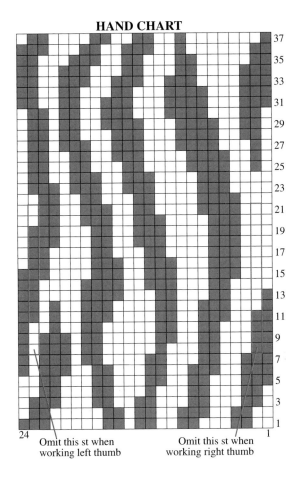

37
35
33
31
29
27
25
23
21
19
17
15
13
11
9
7
5
3
1

24

1

Omit this st when
working left thumb

Omit this st when
working right thumb

Color and stitch key

☒ St between markers
for thumb gore on Rnd 7

⬛ Black (A)

☐ White (B)

POM-POM MITTENS

For little hands

Brightly-colored mittens in a confetti stitch pattern are trimmed with ruffles and multi-colored pom-poms. Easy two-needle technique makes them a snap to knit. Designed by Jacqueline Van Dillen.

SIZES
One size fits Child's 3-4 years.

MATERIALS
▪ 1 1¾oz/50g ball (each approx 102yd/95m) each of Dale of Norway *Free Style* (wool③) each in #4417 pink (A), #4018 red (B) and #3227 orange (C)
▪ One pair size 7 (4.5mm) straight needles *or size to obtain gauge*

GAUGE
21 sts and 24 rows to 4"/10cm over St st using size 7 (4.5mm) needles.
Take time to check gauge.

RIGHT MITTEN
With A, cast on 85 sts.
Row I Knit.
Row 2 (RS) K2tog, [yo, k4, SK2P, k4, yo, SK2P] 5 times, yo, k4, SK2P, k4, yo, SKP.
Row 3 and all WS rows Purl.
Row 4 K2tog, [yo, k3, SK2P, k3, yo, SK2P] 5 times, yo, k3, SK2P, k3, yo, SKP.
Row 6 K2tog, [yo, k2, SK2P, k2, yo, SK2P] 5 times, yo, k2, SK2P, k2, yo, SKP.
Row 8 K2tog, [yo, k1, SK2P, k1, yo, SK2P] 5 times, yo, k1, SK2P, k1, yo, SKP—37 sts.
Row 9 [P3, p2tog] 7 times, p2—30 sts.
Change to B and work in k1, p1 rib for 4 rows, inc 4 sts evenly across last WS row—34 sts.

Beg charts
Row I (RS) With C, foll chart row 1 for palm of hand over first 17 sts, for back of hand over last 17 sts. Cont to foll charts in this way, rep rows 1-4 of charts, until 10 rows are worked in chart pats.

Thumb opening
Next row (RS) Sl next 7 sts to contrast yarn strand for thumb, cast on 7 sts over these sts for other side of thumb, k to end. Cont in pat foll chart, on all 34 sts for 15 more rows and mitten measures 4"/10cm above rib.

Top shaping
Cont with C only, work as foll:
Dec row [K2tog] 17 times. P 1 row.
Dec row [K2tog] 8 times, k1. P 1 row.
Dec row [K2tog] 4 times, k1.
Cut yarn and draw through rem sts. Fasten off.

Thumb
With A, work 7 sts from yarn strand, pick up and k 8 sts along other edge of thumb—15 sts. Work in St st for 8 rows.
Dec row [K2tog] 4 times. Cut yarn and draw through rem sts. Fasten off.

LEFT MITTEN
Work as for right mitten, only beg chart for back of hand over first 17 sts and for palm of hand over last 17 sts. Also, work thumb opening over last 7 sts.

FINISHING
Block lightly, do not press ribbing. Make 2 2"/5cm pom-poms with all colors and sew to back of hands.

PALM CHART

BACK OF HAND CHART

Color key
▪ Red (B)
▪ Orange (C)

RESOURCES

US RESOURCES

Write to the yarn companies listed below for purchasing and mail-order information.

BAABAJOES WOOL COMPANY
PO Box 260604
Lakewood, CO 80226
www.baabajoeswool.com

BERROCO, INC.
14 Elmdale Road
PO Box 367
Uxbridge, MA 01569

BLUE SKY ALPACAS
PO Box 387
St Francis, MN 55070

BROWN SHEEP CO.,INC.
100662 County Road 16
Mitchell, NE 69357

CLASSIC ELITE YARNS
300A Jackson Street, Bldg. 5
Lowell, MA 01852
www.classiceliteyarns.com

CLECKHEATON
distributed by Plymouth Yarn

COLINETTE YARNS
distributed by
Unique Kolours, Ltd.

DALE OF NORWAY, INC.
N16 W 23390 Stoneridge Drive
Suite A
Waukesha, WI 53188

FILATURA DI CROSA
distributed by
Stacy Charles Collection

GGH
distributed by Muench Yarns

GRIGNASCO
distributed by JCA

JCA
35 Scales Lane
Townsend, MA 01469

K1C2 SOLUTIONS
2220 Eastman Ave. #105
Ventura, CA 93003

KOIGU WOOL DESIGNS
R. R. #1
Williamsford, ON N0H 2V0
Canada

LANE BORGOSESIA
PO Box 217
Colorado Springs, CO 80903

LANG
distributed by Berroco, Inc.

LION BRAND YARNS
34 West 15th Street
New York, NY 10011
www.lionbrand.com

MONDIAL
distributed by
Skacel Collection

MUENCH YARNS
285 Bel Marin Keys Blvd.
Unit J
Novato, CA 94949

NATURALLY
distributed
S. R. Kertzer, Ltd.

PATONS
distributed by Spinrite, Inc.

PLYMOUTH YARN
PO Box 28
Bristol, PA 19007

REYNOLDS
distributed by JCA

ROWAN
distributed by
Westminster Fibers

SCHOELLER ESSLINGER
distributed by
Skacel Collection

SKACEL COLLECTION
PO Box 88110
Seattle, WA 98138-2110

S. R. KERTZER, LTD.
105A Winges Road
Woodbridge, ON L4L 6C2
Canada

STACY CHARLES COLLECTION
1059/1061 Manhattan Ave.
Brooklyn, NY 11222

SPINRITE YARNS, INC.
Box 40
Listowel, ON N4W 3H3
Canada
www.bernat.com

TAHKI IMPORTS, LTD.
11 Graphic Place
Moonachie, NJ 07074
www.tahki.com

UNIQUE KOLOURS
1428 Oak Lane
Downingtown, PA 19335

WESTMINSTER FIBERS
5 Northern Blvd.
Amherst, NH 03031

WOOL PAK YARNS NZ
distributed by Baabajoes Wool Company

CANADIAN RESOURCES

Write to US resources for mail-order availability of yarns not listed.

CLASSIC ELITE YARNS
distributed by
S. R. Kertzer, Ltd.

CLECKHEATON
distributed by Diamond Yarn

COLINETTE YARNS
distributed by Diamond Yarn

DIAMOND YARN
9697 St. Laurent
Montreal, PQ H3L 2N1

ESTELLE DESIGNS & SALES, LTD.
Units 65/67
2220 Midland Ave.
Scarborough, ON M1P 3E6

FILATURA DI CROSA
distributed by Diamond Yarn

GRIGNASCO
distributed by Estelle Designs & Sales, Ltd.

KOIGU WOOL DESIGNS
R. R. #1
Williamsford, ON N0H 2V0

LANG
distributed by
R. Stein Yarn Corp.

PATONS
distributed by
Spinrite, Inc.

R. STEIN YARN CORP.
5800 St-Denis
Suite 303
Montreal, PQ H2S 3L5

ROWAN
distributed by Diamond Yarn

SCHOELLER-ESSLINGER
distributed by
S. R. Kertzer, Ltd.

SPINRITE, INC.
320 Livingstone Ave. S.
Listowel, Ontario N4W 3H3
www.bernat.com

S. R. KERTZER, LTD.
105A Winges Rd.
Woodbridge, ON L4L 6C2

UK RESOURCES

Not all yarns used in this book are available in the UK. For yarns not available, make a comparable substitute or contact the US manufacturer for purchasing and mail-order information.

COATS CRAFTS UK
distributors of Patons
PO Box 22
The Lingfield Estate
Darlington
Co Durham DL1 1YQ
Tel: 01325-365457

COLINETTE YARNS, LTD.
Units 2-5
Banwy Industrial Estate
Llanfair Caereinion
Powys SY21 OSG
Tel: 01938-810128

ROWAN YARNS
Green Lane Mill
Holmfirth
West Yorks HD7 1RW
Tel: 01484-681881

SILKSTONE
12 Market Place
Cockermouth
Cumbria, CA13 9NQ
Tel: 01900-821052

VOGUE KNITTING MITTENS & GLOVES

Editor-in-Chief
TRISHA MALCOLM

Art Director
CHRISTINE LIPERT

Senior Editor
CARLA S. SCOTT

Managing Editor
DARYL BROWER

Instruction Editor
MARI LYNN PATRICK

Technical Illustration Editor/
Page Layout
ELIZABETH BERRY

Knitting Coordinator
JEAN GUIRGUIS

Yarn Coordinator
VERONICA MANNO

Instructions Coordinator
CHARLOTTE PARRY

Editorial Coordinators
KATHLEEN KELLY
ELLEN LESPERANCE

Photography
BRIAN KRAUS, NYC
Photographed at Butterick Studios

Project Director
CAROLINE POLITI

Production Managers
LILLIAN ESPOSITO
WINNIE HINISH

Publishing Consultant
MIKE SHATZKIN, THE IDEALOGICAL COMPANY

President and CEO, Butterick® Company, Inc
JAY H. STEIN

Executive Vice President and Publisher, Butterick® Company, Inc
ART JOINNIDES